OPERATION
SEA ANGLER
THE SECOND WAVE

OPERATION
SEA ANGLER
THE SECOND WAVE

MIKE LADLE AND STEVE PITTS

ADLARD COLES NAUTICAL

BLOOMSBURY

LONDON • NEW DELHI • NEW YORK • SYDNEY

Contents

Published by Adlard Coles Nautical
an imprint of Bloomsbury Publishing Plc
50 Bedford Square, London WC1B 3DP
www.adlardcoles.com

Copyright © Mike Ladle and Steve Pitts 2013

First published by Adlard Coles Nautical in 2013

ISBN 978-1-4081-8787-6
ePub 978-1-4081-8788-3
ePDF 978-1-4081-8789-0

The right of the authors to be identified as the
authors of this work has been asserted by them
in accordance with the Copyright, Designs and
Patents Act, 1988.

A CIP catalogue record for this book is available
from the British Library.

This book is produced using paper that is made
from wood grown in managed, sustainable forests.
It is natural, renewable and recyclable. The logging
and manufacturing processes conform to the
environmental regulations of the country of origin.

Typeset in 10.5 pt Baskerville by Susan McIntyre
Printed and bound in China by C&C Offset Printing Co

Note: while all reasonable care has been taken in
the publication of this book, the publisher takes no
responsibility for the use of the methods or products
described in the book.

Foreword

I first met Mike Ladle almost 30 years ago when this book's prequel was published. The book founded a revolution in our approach to sea angling. By translating the observations of fisheries scientists and their own experiences as lifelong anglers into practical tactics, Mike and his pals paved the way for saltwater lure and fly fishing to become widely accepted as mainstream methods. It has taken a while, but that revolution is now truly gathering pace.

Since then, inevitably, things have changed. For a start, everyone has done a lot more fishing and equipment has improved almost beyond belief. Above all, there has been some stunning new research into the behaviour of the fish around our shores, which is presented in this new edition. Every keen sea angler will be able to use this revealing information to hone tactics and enhance catches.

In these days of climate change, pollution, over-fishing and declining stocks, if you want to be a really successful saltwater angler you need an edge and, although the authors do not pretend to catch fish on every trip (who does?), year after year they enjoy amazing sport with a range of species. Bass, cod, bream, wrasse, plaice, rays, mullet and mackerel are just a few of the fish that can provide fantastic action by applying some simple changes to tackle and tactics. Whatever your interest – beach casting, boat fishing, fly fishing, spinning, float fishing, jigging, livebaiting, trolling or free-lining – there is something to be gained by knowing a bit more about the fish you seek.

Of course, using decent gear and handling your tackle skilfully will always be useful assets, but the truth is that you don't need to be a tournament caster or a millionaire to catch plenty of good fish. Rarely is the latest fancy rig, expensive Japanese lure or fashionable rod the secret to success. More often a minor variation in where, when or how you fish can make all the difference to your catches. Whether you take your rod to the sea every day or once or twice a year, at home or on family holidays, this book will reduce the number of blanks and improve the quality of your catches. Above all, it will give you a good read and a feeling as near to wetting a line in the sea as you can get without leaving your house.

Tight lines,

Mel Russ (Editor, *Sea Angler*)

Acknowledgements

It would be remiss not to give credit to the anglers who, over the years, have shared their knowledge with us on all manner of fishing topics. Thanks also to all the pals with whom we have fished since we were young lads – for the friendship, the fun, the banter, the disasters and the times shared in pursuit of fish.

We would also like to thank all the scientists and researchers whose ideas and hard graft have provided so much food for thought.

We are indebted to our angling friends who have kindly donated photos to complement our own. Thanks to Andy, Austen, Bill, Chris, Clive, Jansen, Kim, Silas and Steve, and to *Sea Angler* magazine for pictures and to its editor, Mel Russ, who was kind enough to write us a foreword for this book.

We are very grateful to Adlard Coles Nautical for having faith in this book, particularly to Liz Multon, without whose tireless efforts it would never have found its way into print.

We would, of course, not be writing this, were it not for the support and encouragement of our families. To our wives, Lilian and Lyn, we say thanks for your patience and tolerance of our nocturnal habits – including the 03:00 alarm calls and for keeping the bed warm when we crept in (often smelling of fish and rotting seaweed) well past midnight. For all the packed lunches, the flasks of coffee and the 'dinner's in the oven'. For the lawns that went unmown, the doors that went unpainted and the other jobs left for later. For allowing us the indulgence of our boys' fishing trips away and for coming with us on some of our overseas adventures – lesser women would have divorced us long ago! A special thank you is due to Lilian who womanfully read and suggested many alterations to the entire manuscript. Any errors that remain are, of course, ours.

Good fishing one and all!

Mike and Steve

chapter_**01**

BASS
EVERYMAN'S FISH

Where the bass are

Along Dorset's Purbeck coast, where we have done much of our fishing, we are well used to cliff falls. The grey shale, interleaved with its massive bands of limestone, is always collapsing under the effects of waves, weather and Old Father Time. Those of us who fish the shores are constantly wary of falling stones and most anglers can tell of at least a few near-squeaks. Mike has had a fly rod and a spinning rod chopped off by falling shale as they lay on the beach behind him and he still has a hard hat, which he occasionally wears on visits to particularly dangerous spots (the same one he is wearing on the cover of the original *Operation Sea Angler*.

From the beach fisherman's point of view, the other problem about crumbling cliffs is simply getting down to the shore. It is one thing to clamber or even to abseil down a hard rocky cliff face, but quite another to risk life and limb by scrambling about on overhanging ledges composed of loose shale. Only those with a death wish would be foolish enough to venture on such a climb. In fact, along many miles of good, fishy shoreline, there are very few tracks down to the beach. Until a few years ago we regularly used one precarious path. It was a wet, steep, slippery and muddy slither down and took a two-mile hike along the cliff top just to get there, but on the right tide and time of day the fishing could be spectacular.

At the foot of the winding cliff path, a short stroll over the boulders gave access to a flat rocky ledge where large shoals of bass often congregated at high water springs. A little further along was a shingle-backed bay that fished well at low water. Big bass scoured the strand line for food and could sometimes be tempted with a free-lined squid or sandeel. At high tide, the grey mullet gathered in thousands to feed on seaweed fly maggots. In fact, many years

Cliff falls along much of the Purbeck coast are frequent and dangerous.

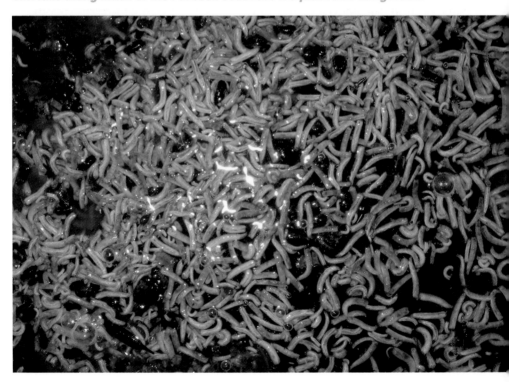

Seaweed fly maggots: tiny but beloved of bass and mullet.

ago, this was the first spot to which we took a magazine photographer in search of fly-caught mullet.

Back then we were called mad to even try to catch the much misunderstood mullet, but the photos of several 5 lb fish that accompanied the article in

> Bass shoals may be very localised, sometimes venturing right to the water's edge.

Sea Angler magazine later that year were proof that it could be done. Wrasse, which were sometimes very large, were regularly caught on plugs cast on light lines and were also prolific.

All of this 'secret' coastline was available to us until, some years ago, a massive cliff fall totally demolished the path. Since then, access from the land has been quite impossible, except by walking along the shore on the very lowest tides. Of course, this results in being cut off on the flood and involves a long stay until the following low water allows you to return. Such trips have, in consequence, been severely limited.

For a few years we have been doing a bit of fishing from a centre console sports boat. Some of this has involved slow trolling over shallow reefs and ledges, but our favourite approach is casting lures from the boat. Bass spend a lot of time very close to the shoreline and these are also the places haunted by big ballan wrasse. One good method is to motor uptide, set the boat drifting parallel to the beach and cast a plug towards the rocks. It is the mirror image of plugging from the beach. You are fishing exactly the same water that you would by casting from the shore, but it is easy to cover spots that are normally inaccessible. This brings us to the point of the story. Suddenly, our special beach, for years cut off by the cliff fall, is again fishable.

When, a few years ago now, we tried it for the first time it was a revelation. It was a beautiful calm evening and the sun was still well up in the sky as we left the little slipway. We motored quickly along to the point where the cliff had collapsed and cut the engine about 50 yards from the shore. The tide was flowing steadily and there was no breeze so we drifted steadily along, controlling the drift with a little electric trolling motor powered by a big caravan battery. It was almost high water and little waves were churning at the foot of the cliff, turning the clear water into grey silty soup in a strip about three yards wide, along the edge of the sea. Cast and retrieve, cast and retrieve – apart from a small wrasse that took Mike's plug on the third cast, there was no sign of life. The gin-clear water could have been devoid of fish. Beneath the hull every frond of weed and limpet-covered boulder were clearly visible. We had drifted perhaps 200 yards when Mike glanced up to see that we were approaching the flat ledge where he had caught bass from the shore, years before.

He called to me and I acknowledged with a nod as Mike flicked his little 3 in black-and-silver jointed Rapala countdown plug towards the rocks. It was heavier than his usual buoyant plugs and went out like a bullet. Mike had used a little too much force on the cast and the lure actually bounced off the rocks before dropping back into the murky fringe of water. Wallop! The carp rod bowed over as the lure was grabbed by a fish that splashed wildly on the surface before tearing away along the shore. Typical bass behaviour!

As Mike played the bass towards the boat I began to reel in my J13 to clear the way, but before I had made two turns of the handle a fish took the plug. Neither bass was a monster (two or three pounds) and it was not long before they were unhooked and returned. Again we cast towards the ledge and once more we were both into fish – superb!

In the course of that evening we managed to set up only three drifts. Each time, as the boat reached the ledge, we caught bass. The rest of the drift (probably half a mile) produced only one tiddler bass and numerous small wrasse.

We expect that you are asking yourself: why didn't they stick to the spot where the fish were? Since it was our first boat trip to the area, we were keen to explore and did not know whether there might be bass or wrasse in other spots. We did learn quite a lot from that evening's events though. The bass shoal was very localised and the fish were only at the water's edge.

When you are shore fishing you can never be sure whether a longer cast may produce more bites. The natural instinct is to cast to the horizon, but – in this case at least – now we knew that the bass were literally less than a rod length out from the beach. On many, many occasions, before and since, we have marvelled at how close in bass will feed and along our stretch of coast that also means in very shallow water – sometimes barely enough to cover the backs of the fish. Whether you are fishing from the shore or from a boat, it is crucial to find where the fish are feeding and, in many places, they may be a lot closer to you than you think.

A good bass foraging in the margins – much more common than you may think. Picture: Bill Fagg.

Time of year

Sometimes it does us good to look back in our diaries and see whether things have changed and to remind ourselves of things we had forgotten. In 1989 most of the summer was devoted to the pursuit of thin-lipped mullet in the local river. We had to think very hard about the habits of the fish and the methods needed to catch them because, despite having caught a great many of their thick-lipped cousins in the sea, our experience of thin-lips (at that time) was meagre. The whole experience proved to be a challenge and occupied most of our fishing time. In fact, it was only in the following season that we turned our thoughts back to real salt water and, after a few exploratory trips, decided to make a concerted effort to catch one or two decent fish before the winter set in.

Although autumn was well advanced, the seas had been and still were unseasonably calm and clear. Local reports suggested that a few bass were being caught on bottom-fished baits, but since many of these catches were small fish there seemed little point in copying such tactics before the weather broke. We opted for the spinning methods which had served us well in former years and which would provide the chance to explore a wide range of venues in a fairly short amount of time. The idea was that, even if we caught little, we might gain a few ideas about where to fish our baits when the autumnal storms finally arrived.

The following account is taken from Mike's diary and should give a reasonable idea of what can be expected in September/October, by anyone with the confidence to employ similar methods, in the sort of situations to be found along many stretches of our south and west coasts (in fact, anywhere that the same species of fish which we caught are to be found). The report covers one calendar week, during which intensive fishing had to be fitted in around work and family commitments.

Day 1

Spent two hours walking the shoreline with my spinning gear (11 ft carp rod, fixed-spool reel and 8 lb mono line) and fly tackle (9 ft 6 in trout rod and number 7 floating line) in search of bass or mullet activity. Passed several other anglers fishing the same stretch of rocks, mostly with legered rag, fish or squid. No one was catching much apart from a few modest wrasse on the worms, although conditions looked good – high water spring tides just before dusk and a little colour in the water. Half a mile from my starting point I found a decent-sized shoal of mullet feeding on the top, but 20 minutes of frantic casting with the maggot-fly produced only one pull which I missed on the strike. The sunset was fantastic, casting an orange glow over the calm sea and tall cliffs.

Day 2

Rose at 05:45 and fished for two hours before returning for breakfast and then work. Arrived on the shore at 06:15 and walked in the opposite direction to the previous evening, again carrying both fly and spinning rods.

Following a ten-minute hike I came across my pal Paul who had similar ideas to me. Paul was already casting a J11 Rapala plug in the hope of bass, but had so far seen nothing. He said that on the previous evening he had caught a decent mullet on the fly at the spot where we met.

After a chat I walked on round the headland into the next bay. It was almost high water and, although there was a good-sized heap of weed laced with maggots, there was no sign of mullet so I decided to copy Paul and spin a J11. Soon after starting I hooked and landed a pollack smaller than my lure. In the next hour and a half, ten wrasse took the plug, with the biggest perhaps 2 lb. Between the sixth and seventh wrasse two bass of roughly the same size were landed and returned. A bigger bass had a look at the lure but found it wanting. I returned to find that Paul was just packing in, having landed another decent mullet on the fly.

In the evening, just before sunset, I returned to the spot fished the previous day with local photographer Ken Ayres who was hoping to photograph both sunset and fish; only the sunset materialised. On the way back I dropped in on another bay for a quick look, only to find that it was full of mullet. Returned home fishless but wiser.

Day 3

No sunset this evening (cloudy), but my friend Dave and I both fished for mullet where I had seen them the day before. I missed a couple on the fly, but Dave landed a four-pounder on light float gear and maggots. Ken took a few pictures. Fishing time about two hours.

Day 4

06:00 start. Went along to the place where I had met Paul and fished a J11 Rapala for one and a half hours. Landed two ballan wrasse of about 4 lb each. No other bites. The wrasse really fought hard (at first), but I was sure, because of their characteristic plucking bites, that they were not bass, even before they showed themselves.

Changed lures to a small floating Rebel Crawfish before returning to the car and, on the way back, could not resist a few chucks in a little rocky cove. Was astounded to hook the tiniest bass I have ever caught – no more than 2.5 in long. In the evening I went plugging with Dave and our pal Peter (on holiday for a week). Peter had a small pollack and we landed a couple of mini-wrasse. Saw a school of fish zipping along the surface at dusk but could not catch them. Probably scad?

Day 5

Down on my own again at 06:30. Only able to fish for 30 minutes or so because I needed to be at work early to do some electric fishing in the river. Low water, so I decided to fish a little stretch of a gritty beach by the car park. After about 20 minutes' casting, the Rebel plug was seized by a good fish, which made a huge boil as it took in about 2 ft of water, 15 ft or so from the water's edge. Thought for a second or two that it might be another big wrasse, but after it had dragged about ten yards of line from the reel under maximum pressure I knew it was a bass.

A bass angler's dawn. The rising sun lights up the sky – almost time for a last cast.

As the fish battled towards a wrack-covered ledge I applied side strain and backed away along the beach to try to turn it – success! After three or four more surging runs, interspersed with bouts of heavy surface thrashing, I saw the deep flank and brassy gill cover of the fish as it wallowed in the shallow water. I bent the rod and slid the head of the fish onto the fine shingle before picking it up and carrying it up the shore. I laid the bass on the pebbles and killed it before removing the treble hooks. (It weighed 8 lb 7 oz and was the only one I kept that year.)

Day 6

Dave picked me up at 05:30 and we went to collect Peter for his last fishing session before he had to catch the train home. He told us that he had lost a decent bass on legered mackerel head the previous evening. We drove down to the sea and met Steve (by chance) in the car park. The four of us walked along to the spot where I had caught the big wrasse earlier in the week. Just after it became light and as the sun came up Steve had a good wrasse on a Rapala J11. By now Dave had wandered off to fresh fields, but the three of us continued spinning and I was next to score with another fair-sized wrasse, then a small one, followed last of all by another big one. We packed in and returned well pleased with the session.

So that was Mike's week of intensive spinning, a total of 11.5 fishing hours which produced a small pollack, 16 wrasse (including three of around 4 lb each) and four bass, ranging from less than 1 oz to just under 8.5 lb. Perhaps he could have caught more or bigger fish by choosing his spots more methodically and by fishing bait, but he certainly covered a fair bit of ground and recounts that he learned a few things that stood him in good stead before the summer fish left for their winter quarters.

Since that autumn the tackle and methods have changed a bit – braid instead of nylon mono line, poppers and soft plastics as well as plugs and woodlouse flies for the bass and mullet when conditions are right – but that is progress.

Time of day

It is noteworthy that much of our best fishing has been around dawn and dusk – why should this be? It is worth looking at one example: sandeels are one of the most common foods of many of our sea fish, including bass. Because these little fish are so abundant and often swim near the surface of the sea during daylight hours, they are also eaten by many sea birds, notably smaller species such as terns, guillemots and razorbills. In fact, sandeels are so important to the diet of certain birds that the breeding success of the birds seems to depend largely on the abundance of these little fish. In the 1980s there was a notable catastrophic breeding failure of Arctic terns in the Shetland Islands that seemed to be caused by commercial over-fishing of sandeel stocks. Netting is not the only problem for these fish; their burrowing habit makes them particularly vulnerable to pollution by the sediments in which they live and oil spills are a real killer.

From an angler's point of view, the sandeel is excellent bait for many species. Not only are the natural eels sold and used to bait hooks, but many of the artificial lures and flies are designed specifically to imitate these slim silvery fish. Clearly, if we are to target sandeel predators (in our case bass, mackerel and pollack), it would be useful to know more about the habits and behaviour of sandeels themselves.

The marine scientist Dr. P. Winslade has studied the life of the lesser sandeel, one of our most common species. He used a photographic method to record the activities of captive lesser sandeels. These fish breed in the autumn, and after spawning they remain buried (and presumably inaccessible to most predatory fish) in the sandy seabed until April. As the water warms up, the fish begin to emerge to feed on plankton during daylight hours. They return to their sandy retreat every night. This feeding behaviour continues until about August when once again the fish withdraw into the sand for a long autumn and winter rest. By observing the fish at a range of temperatures Winslade showed that they are not active at 5°C, but at water temperatures of 10–15°C they feed very actively in daylight hours.

Lesser sandeels become active above 10°C and are only available to most predatory fish during daylight hours between April and August.

So lesser sandeels are only available to fish during daylight between April and August. However, the real key to using these fish as bait is their vulnerability as they emerge from their hiding places at dawn and when they return at dusk.

> **Predation on sandeels is almost entirely concentrated in the short periods of transition between day and night.**

Studies on a Pacific Ocean species of sandeel by Dr. E. S. Hobson of the fisheries laboratory in Tiburon, California, revealed the secret. He observed the eels while he was diving at dusk in a cove with a mixed bottom of rocks, shingle and sand. The eels in question were 4–6 in long and, just like our own lesser sandeel, spend the hours of darkness buried in the sand. Like our fish, they are attacked by a variety of predators when they are in open water. In fact, it was found that the predation was almost entirely concentrated in the short periods of transition between day and night. For practical reasons most of the observations were made at dusk, but it is certain that the same story applies at dawn, possibly even more so, because many predators are likely to be hungry after a night of fasting.

The night-time refuge for the eels was a single patch of coarse, gritty sand. When the sand was disturbed (by the scientist) the buried sandeels became agitated and swam up before diving into the sand again. By counting the numbers disturbed it was shown that at least some were buried at all times.

Lesser sandeel on a conventional rig with ball weight and long shanked hook. Picture: Sea Angler magazine.

However, only a very few were in the sand during the day. At night the sand was stuffed with eels.

In daylight the sandeels foraged for food in the strong currents at the mouth of the cove, but about 30 minutes before sunset the little fish gathered in tight schools just above the seabed over their favourite patch of sand. These same patterns of behaviour have been shown for our own sandeels.

The first thing to note is that, although sunset was at about 22:00, underwater there was less light and the schools of sandeels were beginning to make dummy runs towards the sand by about 20:30. Every so often, as the schools approached within a yard of the seabed, small numbers of eels would peel off and dive into the sand. It was at this time that the predators – rock sole, starry flounder, great sculpin and eelpout (read this as turbot, brill, bass and whiting if you want) – began to gather in the area. The most interesting thing from the angler's point of view is that the predators gathered over the same spot and at the same time as the sandeels.

> About 30 minutes before sunset the little sandeels gather in tight schools just above the seabed.

The four species of predatory fish all swam beneath the sandeel shoal and only tried to catch burrowing eels (presumably the free-swimming eels were too nippy to be caught). The sole and flounder watched for puffs of sand disturbed by uneasy sandeels and attacked by driving their protrusible jaws into the sand that was kicked up by them.

In contrast, the bullhead and eelpout struck only at sandeels which, having burrowed in an unsuitable spot, were emerging before swimming elsewhere. These dissatisfied eels often paused briefly with their heads out of the sand. Frequently, that was their last mistake – the predators attacked as soon as they appeared. Presumably this behaviour is even more obvious at dawn when all the eels are re-emerging. Once properly buried, the sandeels were safe and secure. The predation continued until well after sunset (up to 22:30), after which the predators dispersed.

Vulnerability of bait fish to predators at the change of light has mostly been observed in the tropics where, because of the rapid sunrise and sunset, it is more short-lived and closer to the actual setting and rising of the sun than in our temperate latitudes. Nevertheless, it seems that, in the seas around the UK, although you can catch bass and other predatory fish at all hours of day and night, there are probably short spells at dusk and dawn when the fishing is likely to be red hot.

What can be learned from these simple studies carried out on the other side of the world?

- The predatory fish were local in their distribution. They gathered over one tiny patch of sand in a large cove so it would be vital to fish in the right spot.
- Active feeding on sandeels only took place for a short time, which started as the sun dropped low in the sky.

Each species of predator was looking for a particular signal that marked out vulnerable prey. The signal could be something as simple as a puff of sand or the pointed snout of an eel poking out of the seabed. Each predator's methods of attack were designed to catch prey behaving in a certain way.

Predators gather over the same spots and at the same time as the sandeels.

Mike describes here his own little experiment to demonstrate the effects of changing light on the number of bites:

I'm crackers – I know that. I often fish first thing in the morning. Getting up in the early hours to go fishing is not everyone's cup of tea so why do I do it? I get my fair share of emails telling me how other anglers catch plenty of fish both at night and in the daylight hours so why do I persist with my dawn and dusk approach to fishing? I've often written about the theory of why predatory fish feed best at the change of light, but clearly many people are still not sufficiently convinced by the science to drag themselves out of bed. This week I decided to try to prove my point. Logging a normal fishing session is no use because I would spend valuable fishing time playing, landing and returning fish, and the wasted time would distort the results. Clearly this had to be avoided so I took the hook off my little wedge and replaced it with just a bit of shiny fluff.

To record the results I drew up a table on a sheet of A4 so that I could note how many bites I had on each cast. Down to the coast I went, well before sunrise, armed with my hookless lure and my clipboard (I told you I was crackers). With the clipboard, the pencil and my watch on the rocks behind me I began to cast and retrieve. Every cast went in the same direction and was wound back at the same steady pace. Each time the lure was lifted from the water I filled in a box on my chart with the number of bites on that cast. It was mind-blowingly frustrating, knowing that however active the fish were, I wasn't going to catch anything. I know that the place I fish normally produces pollack, mackerel and bass, often in that order as it gets lighter, but in this case they were just 'bites'.

When I got home I put the numbers on my computer. Of course, I expected to see some sort of pattern in the results, but even I was surprised. I grouped the casts in fives to iron out the element of chance on individual chucks. I plotted a simple graph showing the number of bites per five casts as the light improved from distinctly gloomy to bright sunlight. In the dark – nothing. In the daylight – nothing. Through the period of changing light a rapid rise to a peak of eight bites per five casts at about 06:30, and then steadily tailing off over the following half hour. I would be the last person to want to turn fishing into a science instead of a relaxing hobby, and I know that fishing in the dark and in the middle of the day can be very rewarding, but how about that!

That is fairly convincing and there are a few more simple (fly fishing) experiments of a similar type in chapter 9. It is surprising what you can learn if you give your fishing a bit of thought.

These little marine woodlice are hugely abundant and to bass they are like caviar.

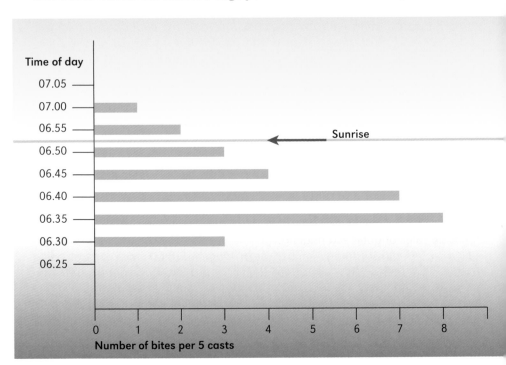

Experiments with a hookless wedge. The peak biting time is well before sunrise and this is why the early bird catches the fish.

In any sort of angling the secret is to know your opponent. Sea anglers, in particular, need a vast store of information about the fish they seek and, while some of this can be gleaned from the pages of books and magazines, what we really need are hard scientific facts. For example:

1   We **KNOW** that in May–June young sandeels are regularly preyed upon by bass as they are swept up and over the 'bow wave' of a seabed reef.

2   We **KNOW** that seaweed fly maggots as they float on the surface during high water spring tides are eaten by mullet and bass.

3   We **KNOW** that, particularly in the autumn, great masses of *Idotea* (sea slaters) attract bass of all sizes into weedy coves.

4   We **KNOW** that big bass can be territorial over intertidal rocks, swimming in as soon as the water is deep enough to cover their backs, driving away rivals from their chosen area and leaving when the tide begins to ebb.

5   We **KNOW** that in rivers thin-lipped mullet swim upstream in spring and autumn to feed on riverbed diatom blooms.

All these things are facts.

Of course (thankfully), there is still a great deal to be learned about how to catch sea fish and much of our approach must continue to be by trial and error. We don't know, for example, why bass will often ignore or reject a juicy bait laying in their path; why thick-lipped mullet often (but not always) ignore the baited spoon while their thin-lipped cousins are easily suckered; or why wrasse will readily take a fish-like plug but hardly ever touch a piece of fish bait. It can be amusing and thought-provoking to speculate on the reasons for such oddities. However, there can be no doubt that a lot of satisfaction (and success) is to be gained by separating the hard facts from the hearsay and speculation.

Timing is, without doubt, the key to angling success, yet very few of us take this important factor into account. So keen are we to wet a line that we often arrive on the beach when the fish just aren't feeding.

Let us give you another example from our own fishing trips to underline the lesson. It proves that, like anyone else, we can get bitten by the bug and forget the basic rules of good sea angling.

Dave and Mike had planned to be fishing by 18:00, their arrival being governed by the time they could get away from work, the time it would take to down their tea and the amount of traffic on the roads. As it turned out they could have worked late, eaten a four-course meal and walked the five miles to the coast. For three and a half hours they saw and caught nothing. Their baited hooks lay untouched on

In the seas around the UK, there are a couple of hours at dusk and dawn when the fishing is likely to be 'hot'.

the seabed and their lures wriggled their enticing way through mile after mile of apparently empty salt water. Even the most enthusiastic sea angler needs a little encouragement in the form of bites or sight of his quarry to keep him alert, so you can understand their flagging concentration after such a long period of inaction.

The sun had just dipped below the horizon as, for the umpteenth time, Mike retrieved his tiny balsa plug between the scattered boulders and gently swaying tufts of bladder wrack. The progress of the plug was easily visible from the moment when it planed beneath the calm surface until it was lifted from the water's edge. He opened the bale arm of the reel and again flicked the lure 15 or 20 yards, straight out to sea. After two or three turns of the handle he switched his mind to 'auto-retrieve' and glanced along the beach to where Dave was tending his free-lined sandeel.

As though the turn of his head was a signal he felt the butt of the rod knock under his hand. Was it a fish? His eyes searched the water for the black form of the plug beneath the surface. It took a couple of seconds to locate the flickering movement and, as he did so, he noticed a fish shape sliding along just behind it. Surely, here was the culprit. The flicker and the following shadow merged and, as they came together, the rod whanged over into its fighting curve and his reel clutch buzzed wildly. Mike turned to shout for Dave's assistance, but Dave was already bounding along the shore, net in hand. At first the fish had the upper hand, but, like most bass, it was prepared to battle it out in open water. So, after a couple of minutes, the continual pressure on the line began to tell.

By now Dave was knee-deep in the clear water with the waiting net well submerged. He watched intently as Mike worked the bass towards him. Every scale on the silver-grey flank was visible as the tired fish came closer. It slid over the rim of the net into the safety of the meshes – 8 lb of pure fighting beauty.

The occasions when the changing light of dusk produced fish are too numerous to recall, but hard scientific evidence of the importance of taking time is difficult to come by. The moral of this story is that whether your favourite fish is bass, cod, pollack, flounder or turbot, one thing is certain – there's little point in chuck-and-chance-it methods and much to be gained by thinking things through.

Livebaits

Sandeels have always been regarded as *the* bass bait and, indeed, fishing a live sandeel is an excellent way to tempt bass. However, anglers around the country have used other species of fish as bass baits, often with considerable success, so we will give our own limited experiences of the matter.

First an example: it was September. Early in the week Mike had a short session fly fishing at dawn. His only bite on the fly turned out to be a very small bass. For the last ten minutes he switched to a popper and had one more bite that he missed, presumably another small bass. Anyway, nothing of note.

Fly-caught mackerel often make good (undamaged) baits.

His next trip was to a rock mark where he expected to catch a range of fish species on the fly gear. For ages we had been saying that we should give livebaits a try for the bass at this spot, largely because the potential baits are often plentiful. Mike lugged along his spinning rod, his fly rod and a float rod set up in the same fashion that we use for pike fishing (but without a wire trace). The rig was simple: just a 4/0 circle hook and a slit wine bottle cork for a float. No weights or swivels.

He set about fly fishing just before first light and his first catch was a bass of well over two pounds – it fought like stink. Then he had a smaller bass and a couple of pollack. His third pollack was tiny (about 5 in) and he decided to try it as livebait. He lip-hooked it and plopped it into the sea. It seemed to be behaving itself, swimming round under the cork a couple of yards beyond the ledge, so he felt that it was safe to pick the fly rod up again. He laid down the float rod, opened the bale-arm and left the little pollack to swim where it wanted. As he fly fished he glanced occasionally at the cork to see that the bait was OK. Suddenly he looked and the cork had gone. His first thought was that the pollack must have pulled it under. Mike picked up the float rod and tried to lift the float – it wasn't there. He reeled in and it was only when he had recovered about 60 ft of line that he saw his float. The pollack was still on the hook, a bit the worse for wear, but still alive. Could the assailant have been a bass?

Shortly after the abortive run Mike caught a modest mackerel on the fly. He replaced the damaged pollack with the mackerel, which promptly set off for the horizon, dragging the cork behind it. No chance of laying the rod down this time so, ignoring the fly tackle, he decided to hold the float rod. Five minutes later the mackerel was still powering away, but after venturing well out to sea it had swum back to within ten yards of where he stood. Although it was easily capable of dragging the little float under, it rarely did, so there was no problem keeping in touch with the bait and the rapid vibrations transmitted through the rod and line showed that it was fit and well. Suddenly the cork went under quite sharply and the line began to stream off his reel. This time it was just a steady powerful pull, very different from the throbbing rhythm of the swimming mackerel. He let the fish run for some time, in fact it probably took 30 or 40 yards of line, before he decided to tighten. His heart was in his mouth as he closed the bale-arm and gently lifted the rod. It was on!

The clutch buzzed as the fish took line against strong resistance. It was a few minutes before he had his bass close to the ledge. He beached it on a wave and had his first decent look – it was well over 6 lb and beautifully hooked in the scissors. The whole scenario was just like the ones we have experienced many times with pike. Was he pleased!

Apart from anything else the bass was much heavier than any that we had ever caught on flies or lures from that spot – perhaps a coincidence? As Mike said at the time, 'I shall be trying the technique again just to prove the point.'

Soon afterwards he had a couple more goes, both short (1–1.5 hours) early-morning sessions. He geared up to bait catching with a small Toby on the end and an uptrace Mylar fly. On the first attempt it was pretty rough (dangerous) and he could not buy a bite from mackerel. Eventually he hooked a garfish on the fly, but by then it was time to go home so he released it.

He went again the following morning and found the sea much calmer. The wind had eased and the swell had gone down. The tide was just beginning to rise when he started fishing at about 06:15. After about ten minutes he had a couple of feeble bites (possibly garfish) and then hooked a splashy little fish, which turned out to be a small schoolie, on the Toby. It fell off into a rock pool so he cast again and promptly hooked a pollack of about 8 in length. Mike released the bass and put the pollack on the livebait rod (circle hook and wine bottle cork float). The pollack swam round gamely for about 15 minutes and nothing happened so he picked up the spinning rod and had another cast. First chuck, the Toby was taken by a mackerel which he reeled in and used as a replacement for the pollack.

By now he was looking at his watch and thinking it was about time he packed in. However, he lowered the mackerel into the sea and let it swim off. For about ten minutes it ploughed along towing the cork behind it and occasionally splashing on the surface. Suddenly Mike felt a hard knock on the rod and the line began to stream off the spool. As he had done before he let the fish take a lot of line before closing the bale-arm and tightening. Again the fish was on!

It was a good scrap, not least when Mike had to land the bass by jumping down onto a lower ledge already awash with the swell. The fish was perfectly hooked in the upper lip and was in fine fat condition. When weighed, it proved to be just under 11.5 lb.

Mackerel livebait, on a circle hook, ready to go. The wine bottle cork float is generally not necessary.

An 11-pounder caught from the shore on a live mackerel.

These were our first two bass on mackerel livebaits. Nigel and Mike tried again the following season and managed to land two more. Neither of them were monsters, but, significantly, both were still much bigger than any we have had on lures from the same spot. It occurred to us that some readers might wonder what the fuss was about. After all, people have been using mackerel livebaits for a long time. Certainly, the late John Darling, a bassing legend, caught big bass on livebaits (armed, if we remember rightly, with a big treble hook attached by a bridle rig stitched through the eye socket of the bait) from his boat and we know that anglers in the Channel Islands have used them from the shore for decades. No doubt, there are many other people who have been catching bass on live mackerel (usually small ones described as 'Joeys') for years.

So what is different about our approach? The truth is – nothing. However, from a personal point of view most of the places that we have traditionally fished for bass are so shallow that mackerel are a rarity and obtaining them for bait would have been virtually impossible. It was only relatively recently (three or four years back) that we started fly fishing in deeper water for mackerel, pollack, scad and bass. It turned out that at these spots catching mackerel was often easy and you did not usually have to wait long for a suitable bait to volunteer its services. We should say that we never bother how big the mackerel is and the first one landed that is in good nick goes on the livebait rod. Of course, there is nothing worse than struggling for ages to catch a bait, particularly if you don't have much time. By fishing early mornings we can generally get a bait in the first few minutes, sometimes on a fly, but especially if we stick a small spoon, a Toby or a wedge on the spinning rod.

Having caught the bait, it is lip-hooked on a circle hook (our pals Nigel and Ben do more or less the same) and set swimming freely (Mike no longer even bothers with a float as mackerel rarely go to ground). The only problem we have had is when we have become bored with holding the rod. On two or three occasions Mike has tied the rod handle to his heavy fishing bag (so there is no risk of it being dragged in, believe me), eased the reel's drag right off and let it fish for itself. Eventually what happens is that the line trails round the kelp (not far under the surface) and the mackerel gets tangled up on the bottom, sometimes resulting in a lost hook (only a hook in this case). If we hold the rod we can keep a more or less tight line and lead the bait around our 'swim' so snagging is never a problem.

Now there must be lots of places (shingle beaches, rocky ledges, breakwaters and piers, for example) where catching mackerel is relatively easy. We have to say that we would have no qualms about sticking one on for bait in such situations. We are certain that if more people tried this approach they would catch a lot more big bass than they do at present. Of course, not everyone wants to wait for hours in the hope of a good fish. Often we are well satisfied with a catch of several modest bass taken on lures or flies and we still have the chance of a decent specimen.

However, it is like anything else: if you want big carp, pike, perch etc. you often need to be patient and avoid the small ones. It also helps if you know that there are big bass about in the spots you fish (we didn't at first).

For some reason live mackerel baits attract much bigger bass than any of the conventional lures. At the time of writing we have had four (and some missed bites) in about 20 man-hours of fishing so it is not quick. Nevertheless, the excitement has to be experienced to be appreciated when you first feel a knock, line starts to pour off the reel and you have no idea whether the taker is 5 lb or 15 lb.

After returning from holiday Mike decided to have another go with the livebaiting tactics. Here is his description:

I have to say it was hard to drag myself out of bed at 04:45 after my 11-hour flight, but I managed to get the gear together and I was on the rocks at about 05:30, just as it began to get light. I took three rods – fly, spinning and livebait – and started fishing with the fly gear to try to catch a mackerel. It was flat calm and the sky was clear, so I was quite hopeful.

My first take, on the fly, turned out to be a decent pollack, but it snagged me in the kelp and eventually came unstuck. A couple of minutes later I was into a mackerel which I managed to land. Now fly-caught mackerel are the best baits because they are easy to unhook and so are less traumatised by being caught. This is quite important because a nice, lively mackerel which has not been handled too much will swim, more or less, for ever. On the other hand, if the bait's mouth or gills have been damaged or if you take too long getting it on to the livebait hook it may only keep going for a few minutes.

Typical squid damage. Squid can be a nuisance, attacking and killing livebaits, particularly after dark.

A squid caught in daytime, on fly gear. These animals are usually much more of a nuisance to anglers using livebaits at dusk and dawn. Picture: Steve Binckes.

As it turned out my fish, free-lined on a 6/0 circle hook, was still swimming hard after about an hour (you'll gather that I didn't have a bite). By now I was getting a bit edgy. I knew that there were lots of fish about (I could see the boils and rings on the surface) so I tied the butt of the rod to my heavy tackle bag and laid the rod down to fish for itself (with the clutch loosened right off in case of a take, ever the optimist!). I picked up the spinning rod and had a chuck with the heavy spoon on the end. Wallop – I was into a bass. Next cast a mackerel, then another bass. I swapped over to the fly rod and had a couple of pollack on the fly. Now I checked the livebait gear only to find that the mackerel had gone to ground (I should never have laid it down). After a bit of a tug of war it came free, but the bait was gone so I packed in and went home.

Now I know I said that livebaits produce bigger bass than lures, but this is the other side of the coin. If I had stuck to spinning and fly fishing I would probably have caught 40 fish or even more in my hour and a half. You can't have it both ways.

As mentioned previously, Mike caught bass of 6 lb and 11 lb on mackerel livebaits on his first real attempts in the autumn. The fish were taken from a spot where we catch hundreds of small bass on lures and flies so he was really pleased to get a couple of decent fish. He was pretty certain that the two big

Circle hooks work well with mackerel fillet, squid and other big baits.

fish were not just flukes, but decided to try to prove the point by a concerted livebaiting effort the following year. Of course, he had no idea whether the bigger fish were there all season or not so he started early on and every trip or two he spent half an hour or so swimming a live mackerel about on a 6/0 circle hook. Time after time he never had so much as a sniff and often had to watch his pals hauling out bass, pollack and mackerel on plugs and flies while he stood holding the bait rod. Needless to say, all the bass caught on lures and flies were the usual size for that place, mostly up to 2 lb, with the odd one a little bit bigger.

Big baits and livebaits definitely sort out the bigger fish.

On one occasion he went down early in the morning with our pals Steve and Nigel. They started fishing at first light and the lads soon had a few mackerel and small bass. As usual Mike put the first mackerel on for bait and set it away to search for a hungry predator.

After catching a couple more mackerel both Steve and Nigel tried the same tactic and for perhaps 20 minutes they were (as had often been the case) biteless. Then, suddenly, Mike's line tightened and began to peel off the spool with a much steadier and more powerful pull than that of the mackerel bait. He called out that he had a bite and the others watched as the line poured out – 10, 20, 30 yards. Time to tighten up? He flicked the bale-arm over and let the fish pull the line tight before slowly raising the rod. The tension increased and he was into a fish. For the next couple of minutes the bass surged away and occasionally boiled on the surface with powerful sweeps of its tail – wonderful stuff. Eventually he was able to slide his fish ashore. It weighed 5.5 lb, no monster, but again much, much bigger than the average bass on a lure from that spot.

So there it is. The proof that was needed of the selective nature of mackerel livebaits for bass. The score at that point was: on lures and flies, hundreds of fish averaging probably less than 2 lb with nothing bigger than 4 lb; on live mackerel, three fish, averaging just under 8 lb, and the biggest was Mike's best bass for some time. Are you convinced? We are.

Of course, the interesting question is why. Why, for example, don't we catch the bigger fish on the plugs and poppers? We know that they will take these artificials because over the years we have caught lots of big bass on exactly the same sort of lures that we are using. It must be something to do with the mackerel livebaits, but what?

They are much bigger than most lures, they are very active and cover the water as well as any lure, giving off the ultimate vibration and flash. They look exactly like a real fish in distress (because they are real fish in distress!) and they probably smell of mackerel. In view of our experiences with pike, we think that the size factor may be the key to it all.

To finish with another little puzzle: it is a well-established fact that the fish (e.g. mackerel) often 'go off' after the sun comes up. We had always assumed that they moved out of range of our shore mark, because they can often still be caught from boats. However, at the end of one session we threw in a few left-over mackerel cuttings and watched what happened. To our amazement, within a few seconds, a shoal of mackerel appeared swimming in and around the cuttings and totally ignored them. What was that about?

We have probably had as much discussion with other anglers about livebaiting tactics for bass as about anything else. The truth is that we don't know enough about it. To be fair, we have caught a great many pike by using livebaits and over the years we have developed our own approach to catching these fascinating predatory fish. Nowadays our standard tactic is to tie a circle hook (2/0–4/0), with the barb flattened, on a length of 15 lb knottable wire (no wire if we are bassing). The livebait is lip-hooked on this and suspended under a slit (with a razor blade) cork adjusted to the appropriate depth for the swim. We often use the same bass spinning rod and reel loaded with braid for this purpose. When we get a bite we simply tighten into the pike and usually the fish is lightly hooked in the scissors.

We like to hold the rod when livebaiting so, unless someone else is fishing with us, this means that there is no spinning or fly fishing at the same time. The consequence is that, even if the bass/mackerel/scad/pollack/garfish are mad on, very little is caught (we occasionally let the bait go and have a flick with the other gear, just to keep us sane).

The weed problem

'It's completely unfishable!' On countless occasions we have uttered or heard those dreaded words. Typically, we have driven down to the coast and had a lengthy walk along the shore only to find that for some reason we could not fish. Usually the problem stems from rough, turbulent seas which have stirred up the seabed and ripped up so much weed that any possibility of dangling a line for bass (or anything else) is out of the question. Legering, float fishing or spinning are impossible because the rig, lure or bait becomes wrapped in huge bundles of 'salad' as soon as it hits the water.

Over the years we have tried a variety of strategies to get round the 'unfishability' problem, but none have ever been 100% satisfactory. Lure fishing is particularly susceptible to the snag/weed syndrome. Plugs armed with treble hooks are almost designed to deliberately catch on any snag or flotsam that is out there. They dredge up every bit of loose weed, catch on waving wrack, snag into fronds of kelp and lodge in every projecting rock ledge with monotonous regularity. Even lures with single hooks such as shads, Redgills and flies are easily rendered useless by snags and drifting fragments of weed. An up-trace swivel may pick up the worst of the stuff, but all it does is to allow a couple of turns of the reel handle as opposed to one or none before the action of your lure is killed stone dead.

The Super Sandra is a fine bass attractor but is not weedless.

Slug-Go lures are weedless and attractive to bass as long as you 'work' them with the rod. Despite the weedless rigging of the lure, this bass is beautifully hooked.

By fishing a weedless, soft plastic lure at snail's pace, bass can be tempted from almost any situation.

In 2009 Mike found what he thinks is almost the perfect solution to this difficulty. For most of the following year he stuck to a single tactic, wherever he fished, and he thinks that he caught as many bass as he has ever done. The approach is simple and effective, allowing even a total novice to spin under the most unfavourable conditions with an excellent chance of catching bass.

Of course, there will be times when the water is calm and clear and free of snags and the fishing is easy, when other lures (plugs, poppers, spoons, shads or flies) may out-fish what we are about to describe, but it seems to us that we would be crackers not to have one of the snagless specials in the bag on every trip. We will let Mike tell the tale:

To explain I must go back in time a few years. Within limits, I'm a great believer in big baits for big fish, so I'm always on the look out for bigger and better lures and for a year or two I've been catching numbers of bass on the 16 cm Delalande Super Sandra, effectively a huge curly-tailed grub. These soft plastics

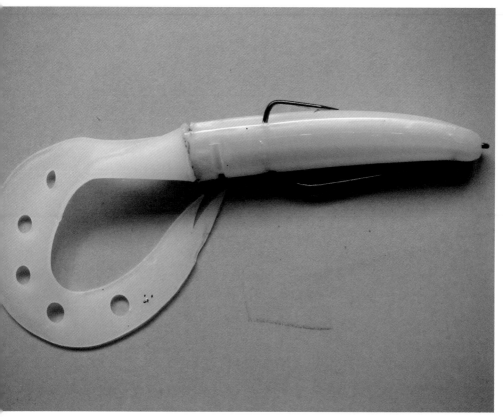

The home-made 'Slandra' is a weedless lure with a good action and is effective even in the hands of inexperienced anglers.

were introduced to me by my friend Malcolm Brindle, a master bass angler. They are chunky enough to cast a fair way, but they are just as badly affected by drifting weed as any other lures. However, I'd found that, unusually, they take bass (and snook and tarpon in the tropics) on the slowest possible retrieve.

Following the success of the Sandras, in 2009 I was given a few of the American-made 'Slug-Go' lures to try out. I could see that these plastics were also likely to catch bass, but since they had no intrinsic movement (waggy or wiggly tails, vanes, etc.) they'd have to be actively worked by movements of the rod and reel. This seemed to confer no advantage over a plug, shad or plastic eel. However, these lures do have one important feature: there is a channel along the back in which the point of their large 'Texposer' hook sits and so is shielded from catching in any weed or snags. I carried a couple in the bag after I got them, waiting for an opportune moment to give them a try.

In the autumn of 2009, on a trip with my pal Dave, he told me that on a recent holiday in Cornwall he had fished a spot with loads of weed in the water. Every lure picked up weed so he gave the Slug-Go a try and, bingo, he caught a couple of bass. He said that the lure had simply slid through all the suspended debris without becoming fouled. We fished together for a time, then I left my pal, still fishing, and began the long trudge back to the car. After a mile or so I

One of several fine bass taken by Marc Ladle on his first attempt with a 'Slandra'.

came across a little gully with lots of floating kelp and other suspended salad in the murky water. I stopped for a look and saw the tail of a good bass right at the edge. After a minute or two I divined that there were half a dozen decent fish feeding in the drifting vegetation, no more than a couple of yards out.

My mind said Slug-Go and I quickly tied one on in place of my plug. First cast there was a bit of a swirl and a tug, which made me think that it might work, but after a few more weed-free chucks and no further action I thought I'd go back to the old faithful Rapala J11 floater. Big mistake! Every cast, within seconds of hitting the water, the plug was clogged up with bits of weed. So I opened the bag, cut off the Rapala, tied on the Slug-Go again, cast out – wallop! I was into a nice fish of 5 lb. The bass fought like hell and it took me some time to subdue and land it. I was extremely chuffed.

I expect that most readers are ahead of me by now. Weedy lure = good action vs weedless lure = no action, so why not combine the two? I tried it. The acid test was on a trip with my son Marc and grandson Ben. Now Ben's a keen angler, but his dad hasn't been fishing for many years so I rigged each of us with different gear. I took the fly rod with a Delta eel attached, Ben had his spinning rod with a bouncy-ball float, followed by a Delta eel on a trace, and Marc, the novice, was given my 4Surespin rod with my new bait attached. I say new bait, in fact it was the hybrid Slug-Go/Sandra that I'd made up that afternoon.

As I've said, for some time I'd been using 'Texas-rigged' soft plastics to avoid weed. I butchered a Slug-Go (front half) and a Super Sandra (back half) and glued them together, producing a weedless, wiggly-tailed lure. This is what I gave Marc, thinking that it would be easy for him to use. The instructions were 'hold up the rod and wind as slowly as you can'. It worked a treat. Marc landed four good bass and missed several more. Young Ben's rig, by contrast, was a nightmare and eventually he lost it wrapped in several pounds of weed.

For the rest of the year I only used my 'Slandra' and caught loads of fish. The advantages are legion:

- They can be fished under any conditions – weed, kelp, drifting debris, shallow water, rocks, day or night.
- They cast reasonably well – 20–30 yards on my braided line (I've caught fish as close as 6 in from the edge in the dark).
- Anyone can use them, even youngsters are pretty safe with a single hidden hook point. Just keep the rod up and wind as slowly as you can.
- The fish take the plastics confidently (some even take violently!) so should hook themselves. QED!

The only real disadvantage is that you have to make the lures yourself. There are possible variations of the idea and some of our pals have been attaching waggy tails instead of Sandra tails to Slug-Gos, producing what they call Slug-Gills – these can be equally effective. Instead of using glue to fix the two parts together, Mike bought himself a model-maker's soldering iron. Heat the cut ends, press them together until they cool and bingo, you have a good, weedless bass lure.

A good bass well hooked on a weedless 'Slandra'.

chapter_02

BREAM AND WRASSE
TOOTHY AND TOUGH

BREAM

Where bream live

Of the eight species of sea bream recorded from UK shores, only the red and black are at all common. Bream are essentially continental species that just about hang on along the south coast. Global warming may change this in the near future and, indeed, species such as gilthead bream are now quite normal catches in parts of the southwest. They have spread from their original stronghold of Salcombe in Devon and are now well established along the beaches and estuaries of the south coast.

The red bream's cycles of fantastic abundance, punctuated by long periods of scarcity, are well documented for the past century. Fisheries scientist Michael Kennedy suggested that a major decline in the 1920s was due to improvements in rough-ground trawling techniques after the First World War. Post-war stocks have never recovered, except briefly, when commercial fishing was halted during the Second World War.

However proud we may be of our ability to catch fish, the impact of anglers on fish stocks is generally negligible. This does not mean that we should slaughter fish with gay abandon. No one is likely to listen to our pleas for restrictions on gillnetting, inshore trawling, purse seining or commercial destruction of small, immature fish if we fail to set an example.

To get down to brass tacks, what do we know about the sea's gamest lightweights, black bream? Their most striking physical features are the deep, compressed, muscular body, the metallic, silver-plated sides and the small head with its neat little mouth armed with sharp, bristle-like teeth. According to ichthyologist Dr. Alwyne Wheeler, in the Mediterranean these fish live over sandy seabeds in meadows of eelgrass, but in our own waters rough ground is their usual haunt.

The contrast of habitats suggests that the nature of the seabed is not too important to these finny fighters. Why should this be? It is obvious that they are not crevice haunters, like the similar-shaped but more ruggedly built wrasse. Their shiny silver camouflage suggests a free-swimming rather than a hide-and-seek existence.

What the black bream eats

A bream's small mouth and set of fine sharp teeth are clearly not designed for shell-cracking, fish-grasping or for bolting large lumps of food. So what are they up to? We have examined the stomach contents of hundreds of good-sized bream caught on rod and line and by far the most common items present were algae. The stomachs were often stuffed with strips of lettuce-like seaweed, presumably plucked from the rocks by the muscular jaws and little, raking teeth.

Anyone who has fished for black bream and felt the hard, knocking bite will realise how well the fish are adapted to tugging-off or uprooting bits of weed from rock or seabed.

Bream are normally considered vegetarians but can be tempted with small baits such as squid strip, ragworm or prawn.

The herbivorous habits of the black bream have been known for many years, but there are also records of them eating small molluscs, shrimps and worms. We have occasionally found little animals in bream guts and the fact that they readily take worm, fish and squid baits suggests that, when the opportunity arises, they will forego their vegetarian existence.

However, the natural preference of bream for plant material gives a hint of how to improve catches. There are documented records of bream gathering in large shoals to feast on grain and other cereals spread on the seabed from sunken cargo ships. This is just the sort of groundbait which is easy to obtain in large amounts (coarse anglers do it all the time) and the bream addict would be well advised to think along these lines. A bucket full of soggy bread laced with particles of crab, fish and the like can work wonders on a bream mark.

The bream season

When it comes to black bream, timing of the fishing season and (if you are there at the right time) positioning of the boat are more critical than in most other types of fishing. The reason for this lies in the regular and precise habits of the fish. The inshore spawning migration takes place in April and, since the largest (male) fish move onto the spawning grounds first (presumably to grab the best territories), anyone wishing to catch these big bream could do worse than to try to anticipate their appearance with a spot of early-season fishing.

A fine male black bream. Nearly all the largest fish are males. Bream can be caught from the shore, but the best bags are generally taken by anglers afloat. Captor: Clive Hodges. Picture: Kim Hodges.

> Both bream and wrasse are able to change sex as they get bigger. Big ones are always males.

Strangely, the fish change sex, starting off as females and later becoming males (just like wrasse do). This odd behaviour provides a reason why, unlike many other fish species, the male bream are usually considerably larger than the females. There is also a striking colour difference, at least during the breeding period. The females tend to have brownish backs and silvery sides, while the males are essentially black and silver with dark stripes on the flanks, a metallic blue cast to the head and a bold yellowish spectacle marking around the forehead and eyes.

When the males arrive inshore they set up 'house' on a suitable bit of seabed, which they clear of loose debris before trying to attract a mate to their nest. After the eggs have been laid the male fish continue to guard their offspring and behave in an aggressive manner to rivals and intruders. This territorial behaviour suggests that, like salmon or trout, they would be susceptible to the use of large attractor spoons fished over the nesting area. A ragworm-baited spoon should be selected for the big male fish under these circumstances.

Sadly, many small bream are landed for sale by continental commercial fishermen. It is generally recognised to be poor fishing policy to remove any species from a population before it has reached maturity and had the chance to breed at least once. In the case of a fish that only produces males at a comparatively large size this is doubly important.

Several other features make the black bream particularly vulnerable to over-fishing. Species such as these living at the northern limits of their distribution are on a knife edge of survival in our waters. The slightest change in climate can result in failure to breed successfully and consequent loss of bigger fish entering the breeding stock at a later date.

The way in which black bream congregate for breeding also makes them susceptible to netting or excessive commercial and recreational rod and line harvesting. In addition, although they were not regarded as good to eat in the past, changes in the eating habits of the public, driven by cookery information in the media, mean that all fish are now liable to be considered as health food. Shifts in the economy and the scarcity of staple food fish such as cod and haddock dictate that, like bass and mullet, bream are offered for sale and will be even more desirable in the future.

Slow-growing fish are more likely to be over-fished than fast growers, so how long does it take a bream to reach a decent size? As far as we know there has been no scientific study of the species, but a male bream of 2 lb 6 oz that Mike caught off St Aldhelm's Head, Dorset, appeared (according to the annual growth lines on its scales) to be 12 years of age. So they are far from fast growers – perhaps their diet of algae is a clue to the bream's slow growth rate.

There we have it, a slow-growing, hermaphrodite, vegetarian fish struggling to make ends meet at the northern limits of its distribution. Is it any wonder that the black bream is susceptible to the worst effects of modern commercial fishing and that the failure of year classes is the rule rather than the exception?

In view of this tale of woe perhaps we should finish on a more cheerful note. A while back our pal Harry told us of a day's boat fishing off Bournemouth. Although plaice were the main quarry, Harry said that it was almost impossible to fish on the bottom without being pestered by small black bream.

These fish are obviously prolific at times and go through cycles of boom and bust, but, given the chance, if they are spared the attentions of foreign and UK trawlers, they eventually become the 2 lb bundles of silver dynamite that we all know and love. Here then is another good candidate for protection as a sport fish. We can but dream.

Circle hooks for bream?

We are now devotees of circle hooks. They are very effective and save the lives of quite a few fish because they lip-hook virtually everything, without the angler needing to strike to set the hook.

A recent innovation is the semi-circle hook, obviously a halfway house developed to try to wean the unbelievers away from their J hooks. The idea is fine, but we were wondering: how do you know whether to strike (like a J hook) or not to strike (like a circle hook)? Due to this dilemma we thought that these hooks might not be all they were cracked up to be. We now have the answer: use them just as you do circle hooks and they should work very well.

One of the common arguments held against circle hooks is that apparently, in the past, some people who tried these devices found it difficult to thread worm baits on them. We are not convinced of this, but using semi-circles should eliminate even this tiny problem. The moment of revelation came in a letter from Mike's correspondent Paul Francis and it is so convincing that we will repeat it here:

Went bream fishing with my brother last Wednesday. Had a very good day, with each of us catching over 30 and most of them of a good size. As an experiment I used Varivas semi-circle hooks, size 2. My brother stuck to his normal (J) ones. Both of us used small squid strips for bait.

As mentioned, each of us caught about the same amount. My brother was striking the bites as normal, but I wasn't. I let the bite develop and just reeled in when they started to make off. To be honest there didn't seem to be any difference in the hook-up rates. We both missed about the same amount of bites.

What was noticeable though was that all of mine were lip-hooked in the corner of the mouth, despite some fish taking a considerable time before they tried to make off. By contrast a lot of my brother's fish were deeply hooked, six of them so deep that he kept them.

As the tide slackened the dreaded pouting came out to play. Again, I didn't strike at the bites and once again they were all hooked in the corner of the mouth.

As the tide picked up again I tried using ragworm to see how things went with wrasse. The hooks were fiddly to put a worm on but not impossible. Once the pouting cleared off I caught a half-dozen wrasse, two of them decent-sized. Again I didn't strike and, the same as the bream and pouting, they were all lip-hooked in the corner of the mouth.

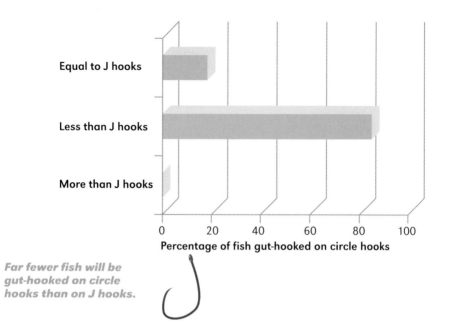

Percentage of fish gut-hooked on circle hooks

Far fewer fish will be gut-hooked on circle hooks than on J hooks.

The only problem I had was that while fighting what was probably a big wrasse the hook snapped at the bend. To be honest I think it was probably a case of the hook having had a lot of hard use during the day and being smaller than what I would normally use for wrasse.

I would certainly use the hooks again and, given that you don't appear to need to strike, I think they will be ideal for uptiding where the lead is anchored and the fish hook up as they move away. They also suited my type of fishing in that I return most of the fish I catch.

I intend to try them out again in a few weeks' time when we go out from Langstone harbour. This time it will be larger sizes and will be trying for smooth hounds with crab bait.

The shrewd ones among you will have noticed the little seed of doubt in Paul's account. Are the hooks he used brittle? (We hate hooks that snap, at least if they straighten you stand a chance of landing the fish.) So we got out the pliers and tried a few – they straightened. It looks as though Paul simply had one badly tempered or fatigued hook (which you can occasionally get with any type). In any case, we are convinced and have already gone over to full circles for all our bait fishing. It saves so many fish being gut-hooked that in our mind there is no contest.

Regular readers of Mike's website may have realised that he thinks that circle hooks are a very effective way of protecting and releasing unwanted fish (he uses them for just about everything). However, in the past, his views were criticised because most of the experimental evidence has been collected from commercial long-line fishing. Recent scientific work suggests that (as we believe) circle hooks are equally effective when used on rod and line.

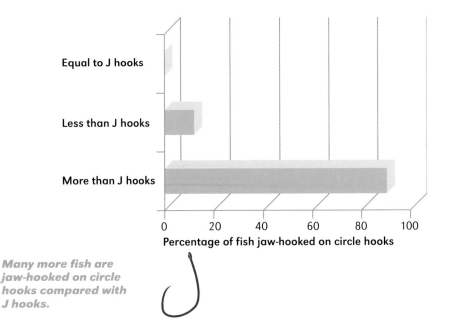

Many more fish are jaw-hooked on circle hooks compared with J hooks.

The info came from Mike's New Zealand pal Alan who is a mine of useful information. He sent a copy of an article by researchers Paul Butcher, Matt Broadhurst, Darren Reynolds and Stuart Cairns dealing with 'fish-friendly' tackle and tactics. Down under, just like us, they are concerned with keeping fish stocks healthy. In some respects they are way ahead because they operate strict size limits and employ catch-and-release for a number of vulnerable marine species of angling importance. Some recent work on their yellowfin bream showed that most angling mortality resulted from gut-hooking. For a start, if the bream were gut-hooked it was much better to leave the hook in (more than 82% survival) than to try to extract it (13% survival). In contrast, 98% of mouth-hooked fish survived when returned.

So the question is: how do you set about consistently mouth-hooking fish? An experiment was carried out with 75 anglers using a wide range of hook patterns. A second experiment involved fish kept in cages and experimentally hooked and released using angler-type tackle. In all, about 2,000 bream were landed and released.

As suggested above, nearly all mouth-hooked fish survived. Over 50% more J hooks were swallowed than circle hooks and the use of bigger hooks also reduced the frequency of gut-hooking. A modified J hook called a 'stop swallow' which had a long bar protecting the gape and point seemed even better at avoiding gut-hooking, but we will reserve judgment on that because it was much less effective at hooking fish.

All in all, it seems that a decent-sized circle hook is not only best for hooking the fish that bite, but it also gives those released a much better chance of survival.

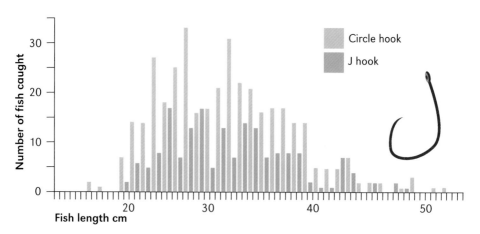

Circle hooks on set lines often catch many more fish than J hooks.

WRASSE

Wrasse behaviour

The fat-bellied, multi-coloured ballan wrasse hunts among the thick kelp fronds that gently sway in the deep, clear waters washing the coastline. Broad, paddle-like fins propel the fish's hefty body, which is armoured with large, loosely attached scales and counter-shaded from dark tones on the back and head to buttercup yellow, orange, white or green underneath. The beautiful colouring is often enhanced by greenish bars and pale spots along the sturdy flanks. The striking thing is that every fish seems to have its own distinctive colouration.

Ballan wrasse have smallish mouths adorned with thick, rubbery turquoise lips, grooved and slotted for flexibility and 'vulcanised' to cope with eating tough-shelled prey. Behind the lips is a set of powerful pearly teeth and deep down in the throat is another group of even stronger pharyngeal (throat) teeth designed to finally grind down its dinner. Truly, the ballan wrasse is perfectly equipped to hunt its shelly victims amid the deep water gullies, rugged rocks and weaving weeds where it chooses to set up home.

> Rarely does a fish hooked on a plug, a spinner or a soft plastic lure escape by seeking refuge beneath weed or rocks.

As a general rule, smaller fish will take worms (with a distinct preference for ragworm), sea slaters (a sort of marine woodlouse), prawns, brittle stars and blue-rayed limpets (those little brown jobs with shining blue stripes that you find sticking to kelp fronds). To avoid the tiddlers and select for the larger specimens you would be well advised to use a bigger hook and decorate it with substantial lumps of hard crab or squat lobster, both of which the big fish relish.

The tough, grooved turquoise lips and pearly white teeth of a ballan wrasse taken on a shallow diving plug.

Traditionally, fishing for wrasse involves lobbing a 1 or 2 oz weight and 2/0 crab-baited hook into a clearing in the middle of a rocky chasm and holding the rod up to keep the line taut between lead and rod point. After a while you feel a sharp tap on the line held between finger and thumb. The tapping is repeated and then the line goes tight and begins to move slowly but steadily to one side – a wrasse has taken the bait in his mouth (all big wrasse are males). You swing the rod into a hard, powerful strike and continue the movement as a sweeping lift. The fish resists and for a few seconds gains line against the tightly set clutch. Quickly you wind down to recover the lost line and heave upwards again.

If you are lucky, the big ballan gives ground and, after a couple of less enthusiastic dives, comes slowly to the surface and rolls on its side, a glowing mixture of bronze and gold. The fish slides over the net and you lift it carefully from the water.

Wrasses of all kinds are tough fish and have an almost magical ability to find shelter in rocky caves or beneath boulders once they feel the restraint of a fishing line. Although a big ballan wrasse will only weigh around 5 lb, under normal circumstances you cannot tackle these bulky beauties on light rods and fine lines. It does not matter if your bait is suspended beneath a float or dangled from a paternoster rig, you will have to use at least 15 or 20 lb line.

Hooks need to be stout, very sharp and selected to match the size of bait, while rods must have plenty of backbone, say a test curve of 2.5–3 lb, to check the first powerful dive to cover, and then to haul the fish clear of its home. That is old-school wrassing.

Ballan wrasse attack artificials with gusto and vary enormously in colour.

Wrasse of all sizes take plugs well, usually by the tail treble.

Wrasse often seize soft plastics and big wrasse will take big lures. This one fell to a 'Slandra'.

Lure fishing for wrasse

Interestingly, there are exceptions to the strong tackle rule. When heavy seas have churned up the seabed large ballans will often leave their rocky haunts to forage over the surrounding patches of sand or grit. At these times, even if you are using bait, a carp rod or light spinning rod and 8 lb line will suffice. Surprisingly, in clear water conditions, similar tackle can also be used for fishing with buoyant plugs, even over the roughest ground. Many good wrasse are caught by plugging every year on the Dorset coast and rarely does a fish hooked in this way escape by seeking refuge beneath weed or rocks.

Although ballans (our largest species of wrasse) are rarely caught on conventional fish baits such as mackerel strip, it is a fact that they are quite partial to the little bullheads or sea scorpions that are so common in rock pools. Since ballans chase swimming creatures (prawns, squat lobsters, small rock fish), it is perhaps hardly surprising that they are susceptible to spun artificials, like plugs, or to jiggled soft plastic lures. Having said that, it probably pays to use drab lures that resemble the natural prey, but fish

> When heavy seas have churned up the seabed large ballans will often leave their rocky haunts to forage over the surrounding sand or grit.

A rock cook wrasse, small but beautifully marked.

A corkwing (top) and a ballan, both taken on ragworm baits.

Note the characteristic greeny-blue and orange stripes under the 'chin' of the corkwing.

will also take shiny metallic-coloured plugs. Of course, hunger may not be the main reason why wrasse take lures and the fish may simply think that they are chasing the intruder from their territory, by nipping at the tail and fins. The very high percentage of wrasse hooked on plugs that are snagged on the tail treble leads us to believe that territorial aggression is a major factor in catching wrasse with artificials.

Anyone wishing to catch wrasse on lures would do well to ensure that their plug or soft plastic has a hook positioned well back, rather than at the head end. In fact, Steve has taken this one step further and, when fishing for wrasse with plugs, he takes off the middle or belly treble as this can snag the fish around the eye. He only uses the tail treble and has not noticed any drop off in hook-up rates at all.

New tactics

There are still some virtually untried methods of catching wrasse. In recent years anglers have begun to use soft plastic jigs with considerable success and they clearly have lots of potential. This new breed of anglers employ ultra-light gear, short rods and lures

Conventional wisdom suggests that to catch large wrasse you should use a big hook and bait it with large lumps of hard crab or squat lobster.

weighing only a fraction of an ounce. They have termed this method 'Light Rock Fishing' or LRF, adapted from the Japanese craze for this type of fishing equipment.

Stepping up the gear (but even then using lines and lures lighter than would have been considered prudent only a few years ago) the next level of approach is known as 'Hard Rock Fishing' or HRF. Nothing to do with a genre of music, but another Japanese import and, perhaps to old cynics like us, another opportunity to sell more glitzy tackle to those with an appetite for such things.

In contrast to the assertion that these are new methods, for many years we have been catching the smaller corkwing wrasse and chunky ballans on our usual bass/pike spinning gear using ragworm-baited mullet spoons. For example, shortly after a session of moderately successful wrassing with crab bait in dirty water, Mike revisited the same spot, again at sunrise. This time he was with another pal, Dr. Stuart Clough. The contrast in conditions could not have been more striking: this time the water was calm and crystal clear, excellent for lure fishing.

They opted for spinning gear and while Mike clipped on a big black-and-silver Rapala plug (J13) with a view to tempting bass, Stuart tried a flashing mullet spoon. A number 5 silver blade, red plastic-beaded body and, at the business end, a Pennell rig baited with a section of ragworm gave him the chance of attracting several species.

It was not long before Mike felt the tug of a fish and, after a short struggle, landed a 2 lb ballan wrasse firmly hooked on the tail treble of the big balsa lure. Shortly afterwards a couple more bites were missed on the plug, but it was not long before Stuart was also in action with a modest ballan that fought well for its size.

Mike walked along the shore, casting as he went. Within only a few minutes a shout from his companion caught his attention. Stuart's carp rod was well bent into a steep curve and Mike hurried back to see if he needed a hand. By the time he arrived a handsome ballan wrasse was already sliding ashore. It weighed 5 lb 8 oz and was quickly returned to the gin-clear water.

In the same season, during a lure fishing session with Mike's pal Will, fishing on a shallow rocky beach with lots of wrack, they landed 15 wrasse on spinning gear and 8 lb line. Mike had three fish, to 3 lb plus, on a buoyant, plastic brown-and-orange crayfish plug, while Will, new to wrassing and fishing by his side, landed 12 wrasse of similar size on a rag-baited Mepps-type spoon. Yes, wrasse are fascinating fish and there is still lots of scope for developing and improving methods of catching them.

Mike has one more tale of wrasse fishing which is of interest because it emphasises the potential of circle hooks:

Circle hooks are wonderful when it comes to catch-and-release fishing. I use them widely for all sorts of bait fishing these days with considerable success. Recently I had an opportunity to give these hooks an airing when I took two of my grandsons fishing. Young Ben, a keen all-round angler, and

Mike's grandson Ben with a ballan wrasse, nicely lip-hooked on a circle hook baited with ragworm.

my eldest grandson, James, came to stay. In anticipation of their visit I had bought a couple of dozen ragworm in order to take the lads wrasse fishing. Unlike Ben (and although he is a couple of years older), James had done hardly any fishing so a catch was essential. The gear was the same as my perch tackle, size 6 circle hooks on light paternosters, this time baited with bits of ragworm.

Despite what I have been told by some anglers we had no problem baiting the circles with worm, it was just a matter of working the bait round the hook with a little care. Bites were fast and furious and in a couple of hours' fishing from the gravel beach at Worbarrow Bay the lads landed 52 fish between them. Again, none of the wrasse were of great size, perhaps a pound and a bit was the biggest. Using a similar technique to perch fishing, after feeling a bite, slowly reeling until the weight of the fish was felt, they had three species: ballan, corkwing and rock cook. Perhaps the really impressive thing was that every one of the fish was lip-hooked! So definitely worth a try.

Yet another colour variant of the ballan wrasse.

Time of the day

Wrasse are active only in daylight, so restrict your fishing to the period between dawn and dusk. Prime time should be just as the sun comes up over the cliff or the horizon because the fish will be hungry, having spent the night fasting as they rested in their rocky holes.

Although wrasse are occasionally caught around most of our coastline they are mainly warm-water fish and are much more abundant in the south and west than elsewhere. For similar reasons they are essentially fish of the summer and autumn. Of course, the term 'warm-water' is relative and many big wrasse are caught well into the winter by anglers legering with big baits over steep, rocky shores. It will already be clear that you must seek wrasse where their favourite foods are abundant, which is usually around rocks and weeds. Deep holes just below the low-water mark are often good wrasse spots when the tide is out.

Fish will feed well even in gin-clear, calm and sunny conditions, but a bit of colour in the water often sharpens their appetites, particularly on the flood. Although there is a temptation to seek out the deepest gullies, it is a fact that very big fish will venture into extremely shallow water, particularly over beds of wrack. A light legered or free-lined crab

Very big ballan wrasse will venture into extremely shallow water.

A black bream caught, by using a jig, from a shore mark in Brittany. Captor: Luke Lewis. Picture: Simon Lewis.

or a carefully worked plug or soft bait will often be seized with enthusiasm in such areas, to be followed by a spectacular, if rather brief, battle.

Wrasse provide excellent sport throughout the day when other fish are often hard to come by and since they make poor eating and take many years to reach their full size, they should always be returned with care. Sadly, many are caught in gillnets and discarded or used as pot bait by commercial fishermen.

Like bass, breams and grey mullets, they are prime candidates for protection from inshore netting and it is high time that they were accepted solely as sport fish.

chapter_**03**

COD, HADDOCK AND LING
GREEDY, BUT DISCERNING

Cod senses

Your toes feel as though they have been refrigerated as you shuffle your booted feet on the wet cobbles of the beach to check that there is still life below the knees. An icy breeze ruffles the oily, swelling surface of the water as it rolls up the gut between the ridges of rock. Dusk approaches and the darkening sea surges between the waving fronds of kelp; 20 yards out in the gully your hook, liberally disguised by kebabed mussels, rolls gently to and fro between the tangled holdfasts.

A sharp nod of the rod-top catches your attention and instantly the cold feet are forgotten. Knock, knock goes the rod again as you lift it from the rest. A solid, plunging resistance meets the strike and the nylon slashes sideways as you lift and reel to draw the fish through the clawing fingers of brown weed. You slide the 4 lb codling onto the dark grey pebbles and, as you remove the 4/0 hook from the corner of the thick-lipped mouth, you admire the perfect mahogany-red mottling of its back and flanks. Another average winter cod from a northeast coast shore mark. But, hang on a minute, let's look a little more closely at this common or garden codling.

How did that chunky little fighter manage to find your half-hidden mussel bait in the subdued, almost non-existent, underwater evening light? Are those big, wet fishy eyes really capable of seeing right through the tangle of inch-thick kelp stems? Are those little double nostrils really that sensitive? What part do the barbel, fins, skin and lateral line organs play in guiding the codling to your bait? Do the low frequency grunts of one hunting cod alert other fish in the area to the presence of food?

A couple of decent cod taken on bait and traditional beach-casting tackle. Cod are incredibly sensitive to some chemicals released by baits.
Picture: Andy Evans.

To some of these questions the answers are still in doubt, but several clues are available to suggest the sequence of events in the cod's hunt for grub. Cod and codling tend to be sociable fish; they often shoal in good numbers over favourable areas of seabed and, at certain times, may collect into large, compact schools for feeding or breeding (ask any trawler skipper). The fish in a school maintain contact with their neighbours visually, so that in poor light or turbid cloudy water they will pack closer together.

They avoid bumping into one another by sensing the vibrations from each other's swimming movements and pick up these changes in pressure through their lateral line system. In the same way they avoid scraping against kelp stems and barnacle-covered rocks. Swimming prawns, Norway lobsters, cuttlefish and fish also give off vibrations which the cod can sense and track down. If visibility is good the movements of potential prey and the twisting and turning of other feeding cod may be seen at some distance.

The senses involving visible light and vibration are only useful to the cod when the food is close enough to give out a detectable signal. At greater distances the sense of smell is much more useful. Like most other fish, the cod has a 'nose' which is used only to perceive chemicals dissolved in the water. On each side of the snout there are a pair of nostrils (nares). Water flows in through one hole and out through the other. Within the nasal chamber dissolved substances are recognised and the information is quickly received and computed by the brain. The cod then takes appropriate action.

A cod searching for food, particularly in dark or murky water, will try to economise on fuel by swimming with the flow of water. If the fish is in luck and has chosen its feeding ground wisely, it may encounter a scent trail of substances drifting downtide from a suitable item of food. If you are well informed and have selected your fishing mark with care, the item of food could be your bait.

If your bait happens to lie to one side of the passing cod shoal it may be possible to draw their attention to it in several ways. The fish are most likely to catch sight of a large, contrasty or moving bait but only at fairly short range. Similarly, a vibrating, swimming or flapping bait or lure will increase the chance of it being found by the cod.

The best bet for attracting distant fish is obviously to send out a chemical signal from the bait or its general vicinity. Over the years we have tried several strategies designed to make the most of the acute chemical senses of the fish and, like most such attempts, the results have never been sufficiently consistent to prove whether our tactics were effective or not. A summary might stimulate others to improve on our ideas (not all of them original, of course).

Firstly, it seemed only sensible to make use of ready-made sources of attraction. Rough weather disturbs and injures many items of fish food and inevitably, bait digging and collecting activities have the same effect. It may pay to fish over suitable ground that has, for example, been extensively dug on the preceding low water.

To enhance or accentuate this effect it is possible to distribute reject-bait or other suitable attractants within the proposed fishing area. Scraps can be dug in or placed under rocks. It is sometimes suggested that groundbait may be placed in canisters or jars, but in our view there is already too much litter on the beaches.

Large baits will generally produce a stronger, more enduring scent trail than smaller ones and it should be an advantage to provide a large surface area from which chemicals will diffuse by slicing up or scoring the bigger pieces. Where long casting is not necessary it can be an advantage to skin or partly skin fish baits such as herring. It is undoubtedly well worth changing baits frequently because the concentration of chemicals passing into the water decreases rapidly following immersion, although a compromise between this and leaving a bait long enough to be hunted down is necessary.

With regard to the attractive properties of dissolved chemicals in the water, it is well established that the extracts of most of the common bait organisms will attract cod and some of them also evoke a strong feeding response in the fish. The fish will detect quite tiny concentrations of a wide range of amino acids.

These responses are by no means as simple as it might appear. Russian scientists have shown that while low concentrations of odours associated with the presence of other cod were attractive, higher concentrations had the reverse effect and repelled the fish. Such results may explain some of the strange observations of scientists studying the chemical senses of the fish and the even stranger experiences of anglers using bait additives.

Territories and behaviour

Every (would-be) successful cod fisher needs to know quite a lot about the behaviour of his quarry. This is equally true for the conger catcher, the dace dangler, the mackerel man and for the person in pursuit of pike. Nevertheless, it is much easier to see the value of a bit of know-how in fishing for a species such as trout in fast-flowing rivers than for most sea fish. Although what we have to say is mainly about cod, a few thoughts about trout make things clearer.

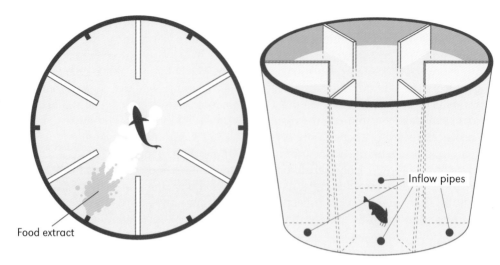

Food extract

Inflow pipes

Plan view of test tank used to show how cod are able to locate tiny quantities of dissolved amino acids.

Side view of tank: whole bait extracts such as lugworm are fed in through tiny nozzles.

We know that trout are territorial because we can see them. A bigger or stronger fish will chase lesser specimens away. All fish try to get the most food while expending as little energy as possible so the biggest, fittest trout will be in the best spot for a regular supply of food. It will be sitting in the shelter of a rock or weed bed where a swift current brings lots of drifting insects past its front door. It follows that the trout angler must cast his fly (or in our case, his plug, minnow or worm) into exactly the right place to entice the biggest fish.

Secondly, trout fly fishermen have described a detailed list of the ways in which a trout will take a fly. A little fish will splash wildly at the surface in its haste to grab a meal, while an older, supposedly wilier, specimen will simply sip the insect in. Fish taking hatching nymphs will make a characteristic bulge at the surface and emerging, drifting or egg-laying flies will each be seized in a recognisable fashion. Any trout angler will tell you that it is essential to understand the basics of these behaviour patterns if you are to catch fish.

So where does this leave us with cod? The facts of life are no different for *Gadus morhua* than for *Salmo trutta*. The biggest, healthiest and fittest fish will be those that hog the best spots and catch the most food. We know that cod and other species will congregate around rocky, weedy outcrops, ledges and wrecks, but these are complicated places. There are many factors involved in this sort of mark: cover to escape from predators, a wide variety of food items, the chance to ambush prey and so on. What about a simpler case where the fish are over a clean sandy or gravelly bottom?

Cod are most likely to catch sight of a large, contrasty or moving bait but only at fairly short range.

Cod will often hunt for sandeels over rippled sand or grit. Places such as the Skerries or the Shambles banks and many other similar fishing grounds around our coasts are good examples.

A fat cod caught from a small boat. Cod are most likely to take moving baits. Captor Steve Richardson. Picture: Austen Goldsmith.

Here the strong tidal currents sweep up huge mounds of coarse grit and shells, which are sculpted by the flow into giant ripple marks. Scientists at the Cefas laboratory in Lowestoft have described the reactions of both wild and captive cod over this type of undulating seabed.

As you might expect, when water flows are slow the cod prefer to swim above the ripple crests. As the flow increases (to more than 2 ft/s) the fish take shelter in the troughs, but only when the ripples are about twice as far apart as the body length of the cod. At very fast flows the fish again emerge from the troughs to swim freely, possibly because the flow is too turbulent for them to shelter.

What does this newly acquired knowledge mean to the boat angler after cod? It is a neap tide, half-flood and the current is running fairly hard so you need about 4 oz of lead on your 20 lb braid. You are in the stern of the boat, anchored uptide of the sand bank. As you pay out the line you feel the weight hit bottom and then you sink and draw to carefully trip the tackle back over the

When water flows are slow the cod prefer to swim above sand ripple crests.

As the flow increases (to more than half a yard per second) the fish take shelter in the troughs.

ridges of sand, up over the crest and down the far side. You feel the lead clunk down into a trough and, wallop, you are into a decent fish. It battles hard and after a few minutes a 20 lb cod is brought to the surface. Several more fish follow, each time the bite comes just as your lead drops into a trough.

Eventually the tide slackens and the bites cease, even though you have reduced your weight to 2 oz just to keep it on the move. You decide to up anchor and drift across the bank with a baited pirk. Straight away the new approach pays dividends, producing another good fish within a couple of minutes. This time the take comes 3 ft or 4 ft above the top of the ridges – magic! A bit of scientific knowledge can be useful at times.

A recent Norwegian study on cod adds a bit more to our file of information. Again the scientists used both wild and captive-reared cod, this time to see how they fed on live fish. The prey used were little two-spotted gobies. Each cod was presented with 15 gobies and given half an hour to eat them. To cut a long story short, both hand-reared and wild cod were not interested in stationary gobies, but both reacted instantly to moving prey. The 'tame' cod were, not surprisingly, less efficient at catching prey and often got involved in an energy-sapping chase. Wild fish, on the other hand, were very smart and simply lunged at the gobies, using much less effort.

Clearly cod that have to capture other fish in the open sea must rapidly develop an effective hunting strategy or they will soon starve to death. This presents a real challenge to farmed cod which are released into the wild – adapt quickly or die. The same problem must face any tame animal that is set free.

What does this bit of science tell anglers about cod fishing? First and foremost that it is hardly ever a good idea to leave your bait stationary on the seabed. Any movement you can impart, either by drifting the boat, fishing sink and draw, cast and retrieve or even by using a long trace which allows the bait to wave about in the current, has got to improve results. Of course, all these things are the basis of good angling, but it is reassuring to know that the tactics you have been using for years (we have assumed that you have been doing this) have a sound basis in the facts of fish behaviour.

> Any movement you can impart to your bait is likely to improve catches of cod.

Cod, haddock and your bait

Let's take another example to show how knowing a bit about fish behaviour can help us catch them. Mike and his pal Harry sat in darkness as the dinghy they were fishing from swung gently at anchor. The oily swell moved the little craft with a slow rocking motion, alternately tightening and easing their nylon monofilament lines (this was long before the arrival of braid) that slanted into the depths from their heavy rods, which projected just beyond the stern.

Reels were set 'on the check' so as to present the least possible resistance to a taking fish. Each of them held a lighter rod across his knees, with the line gripped between finger and thumb as they waited for the bites to come. A light tugging rattle was transmitted up the line to Mike's finger tips. 'Feels like a small pouting,' he said and Harry nodded in agreement. 'I just had one as well,' he retorted. He struck sharply and reeled in a 4 oz pout – they had guessed correctly.

Mike changed his bait and together they lowered their tackles to the seabed once more. Mike's heavier rod dipped sharply and the reel gave a little buzz as it released a few inches of line. A further double knock on the rod was followed by a steady run and he picked up the gear, knocked off the ratchet and felt the line with his left hand. In a series of short bursts, a couple of yards of line trickled through his fingers before he flicked the reel into gear and waited for the line to tighten before striking firmly. 'Must be a conger!' he muttered as he yanked the rod upwards. Sure enough, it was not long before 15 lb of dark grey eel was twisting on the surface by the boat.

The rattle of a pouting, the hard tug of the bream, the knocking drag of a conger or the surging, powerful pull of a bass – nine times out of ten an experienced sea angler will have a pretty good idea of which species has molested his bait simply from the way it sends signals up the line. The big question is what each message really means. Rarely do we have the opportunity to watch a fish as it attempts to take our bait.

Experience may well have taught us to react in a manner likely to produce a well-hooked fish from a given type of bite, but, at best, we must rely on guesswork to tell us what is happening down below. Like most anglers, we have spent hours thinking about how our quarry was likely to approach the tackle and hopefully take the bait or lure, but it was not until relatively recently that some solid information on the matter came our way.

Three Norwegian scientists decided to study the reactions of sea fish (mostly cod and haddock) to baited hooks in the hope that they might be able to advise commercial long-liners how to improve their catches. The results of their work are fascinating to any angler. We will try to describe the main points which came to light.

The experiment involved a short line with four droppers carrying size 5 hooks baited with mackerel strip, set about a foot from the seabed. The water was 22 m deep in the North Sea and observations were made continuously, both day and night, using a video camera and illuminating the area with red lights (which are known not to affect fish as this wavelength is more or less invisible to them).

The average size of the haddock caught was 18 in and the average size of cod 22 in, so most of the fish were sizeable. In an observation period of just over 200 hours, almost 3,000 cod and 860 haddock were viewed by the cameras, roughly 20 fish every hour swimming past the line.

The results are fascinating. In September the cod were active during two periods, one in mid-morning and one in mid-afternoon. In December they were active only around midday. Haddock were active more or less throughout the 24 hours.

Both cod and haddock were most active when the tidal currents were weak, and the great majority of fish, of both species, approached the line slowly from downtide by swimming against the flow. Again, both species swam towards the

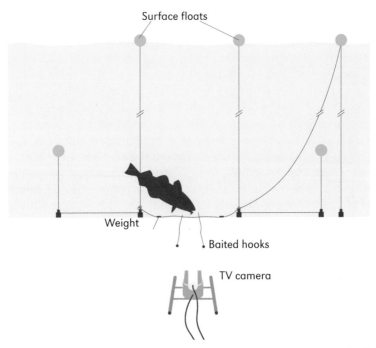

Camera and long-line set up for observing the reactions of cod and haddock to baited hooks.

line just clear of the seabed and the cod typically trailed their sensory fins and barbel across the bottom as they approached.

The scientists describe in some detail the manner in which the fish approached and/or took the baits. They were able to recognise approachers, tasters, partial and complete biters, chewers, pullers, jerkers, shakers, rushers and fish that spat out or otherwise rejected baits – all pretty self-explanatory descriptions, which any angler can identify in terms of types of bite.

Astonishingly the vast majority of the cod and haddock simply ignored the baits. Roughly one-third of haddock and only about one cod in 20 seemed to respond to the presence of the baited hooks in any way at all. Only one haddock in five and just one cod in 60 actually had a go at the baits.

The haddock that did feed often repeatedly attacked a bait, but it was rare for cod to make more than one attempted bite. When cod did bite they were much more aggressive and consequently much more likely to hook themselves.

To our mind, by far the most interesting observation was the way in which cod responded to the presence of other fish. For quite long spells there would be no sign of cod anywhere in the vicinity of the line then, as soon as another fish made a violent movement with the bait (had a grab at the bait or was hooked), 10 or 12 other cod would materialise, as if by magic. Out of all the cod caught, half were hooked while

> **Most cod and haddock ignore baits and attack only when attracted by the movements of a hooked fish.**

another fish was attacking a baited hook. Cod were even seen to attack hooked haddock (not really a surprise).

Of course, there are many other questions we would like answered. Different baits, different depths of water, different species of fish, all would give fascinating information. Despite these limitations, the results of the cod/haddock study tell us a lot regarding how to set about catching these fish.

Quite a lot of cod fishing these days involves fixed tackle, either uptide of an anchored boat or pinned to the sea floor 80–150 yards from the beach. Clearly (from what you have just read) not every cod that swims by is likely to take these static baits, but it seems to us that the best chance of improving catches must be to use a two-hook rig and when a fish is hooked leave it out there until another (hopefully bigger) fish finds the other bait. Similarly, anything you can do to give flash and movement in the vicinity of your bait (i.e. to make it look like a struggling fish) is likely to dramatically improve your catches.

The search for food

The activity patterns in the food-searching behaviour of tagged ling (a cousin of the cod) have been studied by means of a fixed set of three hydrophones, which monitored the position of each individual being tracked once every three minutes. Five ling were acoustically tagged by allowing them to swallow a transmitter wrapped in bait and were observed continuously for 6–11 days afterwards.

The results are interesting. Ling showed much higher levels of swimming activity at dawn and dusk. Each fish occupied what is known as a 'home range' throughout the study. During periods when they were resting (about 65% of the time) they remained within this small core area. Most of the time spent outside the core area was during the period of high activity at dawn. Food-search behaviour was studied by setting mackerel-baited fishing gear in the experimental area. When baits were present, ling moved about more slowly and within a quite limited area, showing that they could detect the presence of the smelly food and were looking for it. Ling responded to and located baits in both their active and inactive periods during the day but were not seen to react at all after dark.

Comparing these findings with those from similar tracking experiments on cod suggest that the ling are less active at night than their cousins and move about less in general. This may reflect different feeding strategies between these two species, with ling taking a higher proportion of active prey and being more dependent on sight to find them.

Clearly, watching fish going about their business can be a very useful thing to do. Imagine having gills instead of lungs and being able to walk about on the seabed and sit down a couple of yards from your baited hook just watching what happened! If you were very patient it might be possible to see the codling, flounders or dabs as they hunted their prey. No doubt you would be surprised when most of the fish passed by your tackle without so much as a sidelong glance. Even the humble lesser spotted dogfish would often turn up their snouts at your cunningly presented offering.

Occasionally, a fish less choosy, more stupid or simply hungrier than the rest might approach your tackle and, if it was really keen, it would grab at the bait and try to rush off with its prize. Feeling the solid resistance of the 6 oz grip lead the potential customer would then have several options. It might decide that the bait was not sufficiently attractive to justify the effort, spit out your offering and move on or, if the bait was a soft one such as worm or mussel, it could rip it off the hook and depart well pleased with its capture. A particularly greedy specimen would possibly hook itself by pulling against the weight, either at the first attempt or, if the bait was both tough and tasty, at the second, third or fourth bite. If your pal, still standing on the beach, was on his toes he might pick up the rod and, hopefully, reel in your hard-won prize.

Of course, it would be possible for you to observe scenes similar to the above if you had a set of scuba gear, but it would need a great deal of time and effort to see anything worthwhile. However, by using modern underwater video equipment, it is now possible to record, for many hours, the behaviour of fish and their responses to baited lines. As described above, video techniques have shown that cod are attracted to baited hooks chiefly by the presence of other feeding or hooked fish, but what most anglers would really like to know is: which is the best bait?

The best bait

Scottish fisheries scientists Johnston and Hawkins used an underwater television camera to test the effectiveness of some different set-line fishing baits. It would have been fascinating if the baits used had been lug, rag, peeler crab, mussel and squid, but, in practice, they studied standard commercial set-lining baits: mussel, squid, mackerel and salted herring. Nevertheless, the results were interesting.

Firstly the camera was run with the line unbaited to see just how many fish wandered by in the absence of any attractant. The line was then baited with one of the experimental baits and the observation was repeated. The change in numbers of fish seen gave an idea of how attractive the various fish found each type of bait. To allow for the loss of baits during the trial all results were adjusted to cover a half-hour period.

For both cod and coalfish, mussel was by far the most attractive of the baits. In the case of cod, mussel was about seven times more attractive than salted herring and almost twice as attractive as either squid or mackerel.

Coalfish were attracted 20 times more often to mussel-baited lines than to those with mackerel on the hooks, and both squid and salt herring came a poor third to the humble shellfish, which was four times more attractive than either.

As might be expected, dogfish did not think much of the mussel baits which, together with salted herring, scored zero as attractants. Mackerel was by far the best for lesser spotted dogs, being ten times as good as squid.

The thing to note, from the results of these experiments at least, is that no single bait was best for all three species.

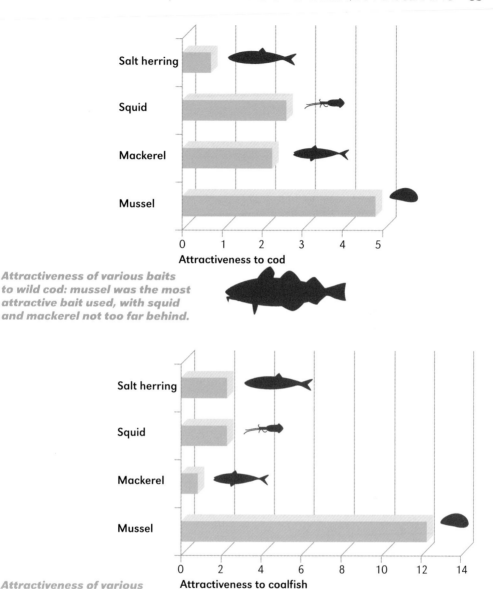

Attractiveness of various baits to wild cod: mussel was the most attractive bait used, with squid and mackerel not too far behind.

Attractiveness of various baits to wild coalfish: mussel was much better than any of the other baits.

Perhaps even more significant was the experiment in which baits were mixed, not as cocktails but on alternate hooks. This showed that mussel, combined with either squid or mackerel, was most attractive to cod and, even more surprising, the mussel/squid combination was 24 times as good as the next best combination (squid/salt herring), even for dogfish.

The fact that fish were attracted to lines carrying a particular bait did not mean that they always attacked the baits and still less that they hooked themselves and were landed. Dogfish never attacked hooks baited with mussel

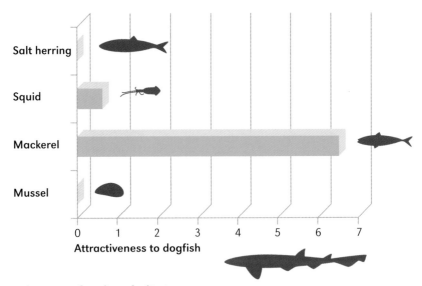

Attractiveness of various baits to wild dogfish: mackerel was head and shoulders above the other baits in this case.

and, surprisingly perhaps, coalfish were not very keen to have a go at mussel baits either. Cod, on the other hand, were equally enthusiastic about grabbing mussel and squid, slightly less keen to take mackerel and definitely dubious when it came to the poor old salted herring. On the long-lines used in the experiments there is, of course, nothing that can be done to hook a fish. Just as on a baited hook, which has been cast 150 yards from the shore or well uptide of the boat and is anchored to the seabed with a hefty wired lead, the fish must hook themselves. Even with tasty mussel baits only about one cod in 12 that attacked the baits was hooked and brought to the surface. As might be expected, a much greater proportion of greedy dogfish were landed – we've all been there!

All in all, this study is a lesson in the inefficiency of waiting for fish to impale themselves on your hooks as opposed to feeling and striking bites. Perhaps it would be a different story if circle hooks were more widely used for static bait fishing.

In another set of experiments a couple of artificially made baits were compared with mussel and mackerel, the idea being to produce a standard long-lining bait which could be used with an automatic baiting machine. The 'synthetic' baits were made of a tough jelly laced with mussel or mackerel extracts. In this case, dabs and dogfish were the main victims. As you might expect, the dogfish still preferred neat mackerel, but, amazingly, the new-fangled baits attracted twice as many dabs as the naturals and induced roughly the same number of bites (attacks).

Again the failings of the standard J fish hook when fished with a static line were revealed. While 80% of biting dogfish were hooked, less than 20%

of the dabs impaled themselves. Well over half of both species were lost on the retrieve.

Cod stocks and survival

Cod are important fish. By now everyone must be aware that the stocks of cod off our coasts have been pushed to the edge of commercial extinction. Just how important are these big-mouthed beauties? Suffice to say that $48 million (£20 million) was the amount spent on cod research by the Canadian government in just five years up to 1994. We all know that governments are so stingy as to make Scrooge look like a benevolent rich uncle, so their politicians must think that *Gadus morhua* (cod to you and me) is a very, very important fish indeed. Yes, it is the same old big-mouthed, pot-bellied, combat-camouflaged, greedy, tasty-with-chips fish that we try to catch from our own shores winter after winter.

Not only is the cod economically valuable, but it is also a key species in the undersea world. Despite the prolific nature of the fish (angling writers delight in telling us that a female cod can lay many millions of eggs), cod stocks have proved to be far from invulnerable. The huge numbers of eggs are laid partly because their chances of survival are so small. A cod larva stands about the same chance of survival to maturity as we do of winning the lottery. In its young stages, even a fierce predatory species such as cod has to watch its back or risk being devoured by something bigger, including its own uncles, aunts or grandparents.

On average, only a few from the millions of eggs produced by a pair of cod will survive to become mature fish. A spot of extra fishing pressure, pollution, starvation or predation and the future survival of Mr and Mrs Cod and their offspring is, to say the least, uncertain.

Even in these days of stock collapse, cod can still be astonishingly abundant. A fairly recent research trip in the northwest Atlantic spotted a shoal 4 miles wide and 20 miles long. With shoals of this size still about it is easy to see why fishermen fail to recognise that stocks are on the brink of disaster. Let's look at just one factor that might be affecting cod abundance. This information is taken from the latest available scientific studies of the species.

The sea temperature has a dramatic effect on the time it takes for eggs and larvae of the cod to develop. A subtle fall of one degree in average temperature can result in greatly delayed hatching of the tiny free-floating cod eggs and massive increases in death rate will follow. Such temperature changes are known to have occurred in recent times.

In the past, the traditional approach to managing depleted stocks of food fish, such as whiting or cod, was to reduce commercial fishing pressures. Increased mesh sizes in nets, the introduction of catch quotas, less hours spent at sea, even complete bans on the landing of particular species have all been tried in vain attempts to halt over-fishing.

Of the 10 million tonnes of fish that are estimated to live in the North Sea, only about 0.5 million tonnes (things are declining so quickly that the latest figures suggest that this is now down to a pathetic 30,000 tonnes) are cod. In the league table of abundance, cod fall well behind sprats, mackerel, Norway pout, coalfish, plaice and sandeels. The latter are by far the greatest weight (almost 1.5 million tonnes). Roughly a quarter to a third of the fish present in the North Sea are landed by commercial fishermen each year and most of the catch consists of popular species like plaice and – yes, you've guessed it – cod.

The massive and relentless impact of modern commercial fishing methods, with sophisticated stern trawls and side-scanning sonar, means that our favourite fish needs protection. In the past, a size limit and net mesh restrictions were sufficient to prevent over-fishing of immature cod, but more recently a quota system has been added. When the quota is reached cod can no longer be landed until the ban is lifted for the following season. In fact, it now looks to us as though only a total ban (or a miracle) will save the cod stocks.

Although cod are widespread in the Atlantic, there are several different races, just like the races of the human population. For example, recent studies with special electronic tags, which record every movement of the tagged fish, have shown that Irish Sea cod are more active and swim over a much greater range of depths than their cousins living in the North Sea. The distinct races of cod live, feed and breed in different set areas so each one may be over-fished independently and must be protected in its own right, even if the fish are abundant elsewhere.

The old and the modern faces of catching cod

At a local level there will also be differences between the fish caught. Any cod angler must have noticed the beautiful coppery-red tones of rock codling and the grey-brown of fish taken from the coloured water or heavy surf on a sandy beach. Fish swimming through the kelp fronds are often orange and mahogany-tinted, while those from muddy areas may be a drab greenish brown or grey. Such colour differences are due to the needs of camouflage and a single fish may change its colour to match the surroundings in the space of only a few minutes. One thing is certain: whether they are dowdy or dandy the cod will always hold a special place in the affections of sea anglers all over the British Isles.

By tagging cod it is possible to discover what proportion of the wild fish are being caught by trawls and gillnets. In the worst situations it seems that well over half of the sizeable fish are caught every year and this is much more than the population can sustain. The first symptom of such over-fishing, as far as anglers are concerned, will usually be a reduction in the average size of fish hooked and landed. This does not mean that you will never catch a big cod, but simply that such catches will happen less often. Are you catching smaller cod than you used to? If you have been fishing as long as we have, we bet that the answer is yes.

The cod becomes most active in dirty water or in the hours of darkness.

On the other hand, you may be quite happy to take home and eat a two- or three-pound fish, but the problem is that instead of a couple of modest fillets in the frying pan you should have been able to feed the entire family from your good fortune, so you have to catch another and another two-pounder to make up the deficit.

There are many more factors that affect the numbers and sizes of our favourite fish. Man is by no means the only species that likes a cod steak. Seals eat huge numbers of cod and squid may devour even more. The short-finned squid specialises in eating cod. In 1979, off Newfoundland alone, the commercial catch of these rapacious cephalopods was 93,000 tonnes – each and every one of them capable of guzzling cod as if there was no tomorrow.

At the other end of the scale, it is believed that there may have been a reduction in the total amount of 'cod food' in the sea. This results in starvation, reduced abundance and changes in distribution of the cod themselves. Of course, there is another side to this. Less cod could be good news for sandeels, whiting and Norway lobsters (scampi), which fall prey to our favourite fish.

So there we have it, the picture of a special fish and a very special breed of angler. Both are active in winter weather, while others, less hardy, lie torpid on the seabed or, in the case of fair-weather anglers, sit at home in front of the telly. The cod themselves range from tiny, greedy, rock-haunting codling to the animated coal-scuttles that lurk in the shelter of wrecked ocean liners or torpedoed cargo vessels. Similarly the men and women who cast a line to catch these prizes, whether in the cold Baltic deeps or from the coaly beaches of the Durham coast, have one thing in common: an intense desire to feel the heavy tugging of their line that signals yet another contest with one of nature's finest creations.

Despite all the doom and gloom we are relatively optimistic. We don't think that we have seen the last of these fantastic creatures. Cod are very resilient fish. They grow very fast (a 15-pounder will be only six years old), reach a large size (5 ft long and weighing 80 or 90 lb) and are capable of rapid increases in numbers once the fishing pressures are reduced. The fish are able to live over just about any sort of seabed. Codfish swim fast and far (easily sustaining 13 miles a day) and are fitted with all the sensory equipment to locate the best concentrations of prey.

Cod hunting

Most people only encounter cod when it arrives covered in batter, served with chips and wrapped in newspaper. Now we would be the last to decry the pleasures of a tasty meal from the sea, but the satisfaction from a cod fillet is so much greater when you caught the fish yourself. If you as an angler are to savour fresh cod with reasonable frequency then it helps to know your quarry.

The cod family is a large one and the cod itself is a typical member. With three soft dorsal fins and two similar ones beneath the body we have a clear indication of a rather advanced design of fish. Other hints of a rather special position in the great kingdom of fishes lie in the powerful jaw muscles and the small, tentacle-like pelvic fins tucked up under the throat. Together with the long chin barbel the fin-tentacles form a triangle of food-locating feelers. The cod is a very adaptable feeder. One minute it may be struggling to pick up and swallow a snapping, armour-plated lobster, the next it will be twisting and turning in pursuit of a fast-swimming sandeel or herring. An instant later it may be turning over the seabed for worms or cockles buried beneath the sand and this is where the feelers come in to action.

The fins and chin barbel of the cod are plastered in taste buds and the fish puts them to good use in the search for food. If food lies covered by sand or gravel, traces of amino acids and other small molecules will leak to the surface, alerting the hunting cod and making it dig for hidden morsels (they can detect some amino acids at less than one part per million).

When its shoalmates see that a lucky individual has left its position in the formation, they go to investigate and come across the finder twisting, turning and flashing in its efforts to obtain the buried food. The fish may then co-operate to dig more quickly, possibly another good reason for using multi-hook tackles in snag-free conditions and not being too hasty to reel in a hooked fish.

In dirty water, or in the hours of darkness, the cod becomes most active. Studies using radio tags have shown that some fish may lie dormant all day but definitely wake up at night. The hunting fish drift or swim along in the direction of the tidal flow, but when they sense the taste of food in the water they turn and swim back against the current, swinging their bodies from side to side, until they find what they are after. Sometimes, if you are lucky, it will be your baited hook.

With all this 'search and destroy' equipment at their disposal it is hardly surprising that cod are greedy and voracious fish. So just what do they eat? The broad answer is just about anything, although they do have certain preferences. If you open up the stomach of a cod that you catch it is a fair bet that you will often find crabs, shrimps, prawns and other hard but wholesome objects within. Molluscs such as whelks are also popular as are large worms such as the furry, iridescent sea mouse, a type of plump, hairy ragworm.

Adult cod tend to eat crustaceans and worms in summer and fish and brittle stars in winter, but they have large appetites and catholic tastes. At times the fish will leave the bottom to forage in mid-water. High on the cod's list of favourite foods are fish of many kinds. Just about any fish which is not too big to swallow is likely to find itself inside that capacious mouth. At certain times of the year the cod may feed almost exclusively on species that are unusually abundant. For example, in winter sprats or herrings are often the main prey.

All of this fits in perfectly with the well-known list of effective cod baits. Crab, squid, whelk, mussel, worms and fish are all killers on their day. Perhaps fish is the most underrated of these because there can be no doubt that small live fish, such as freshly caught pouting, are among the best cod baits of all. It seems that most anglers cannot be bothered to take the extra trouble of catching and using livebaits, even though these may be prime cod tempters.

Cod hunt their food in cold seas. Generally these fish are to be found in water where the temperature ranges from 0–10°C (0°C is the freezing point of fresh water). This means that, throughout the winter, cod can be caught all around the coasts of Britain. The southern limit of their distribution is the Bay of Biscay. In the summer months these fish remain in cool deep water, only venturing inshore when the temperature begins to fall. Generally it is just small codling that are caught from the shore in warm weather.

The feeding behaviour and activity patterns of eight cod in a Norwegian fjord, studied by means of acoustic transmitters, were observed continuously for three to eight days. The scientists were interested in the swimming speed and size of area occupied by the fish. The reactions of the tagged cod to scent was also examined by setting a line baited with mackerel in the study area.

Not all cod slept the daylight hours away. Some searched more actively for food in daylight than they did at night and caught faster-swimming prey in the daytime by using their keen sense of vision. However, the fish also used their excellent sense of smell to locate the baits, even during daylight. The fish were able to detect the scent of mackerel baits from a distance of several hundred yards and at once began to search for the baits by adopting a faster swimming speed.

Cod congregate for spawning in certain favoured areas and most breeding takes place in early spring. At spawning time the cod shoals may be so tightly packed that, on occasions, it is not possible to get a bait down through them. After spawning the new-laid eggs drift near the surface of the sea, usually in areas where the currents set towards the inshore nurseries. The eggs hatch after ten days or more, depending on sea temperatures, and the tiny larvae live on stored yolk for some time. It is only when the little fish are a month old and about one inch long that they swim down to the seabed.

The baby cod occur on similar ground to pollack and coalfish and, feeding greedily, they quickly grow to catchable size. In the North Sea they will reach 14 in in only two years. At a little over three years the cod will be about 2–4 lb and a year later it could be 7 lb or more. Compare this with a bass, which at the same age will still only be about one foot long.

> Cod are able to detect the scent of mackerel baits from a distance of several hundred yards.

What cod want

Cod and whiting, like most other fish, are only too keen to feed on their smaller relatives and many species of the cod family (known as gadoids) are predatory, even to the extent of cannibalism. As they grow, all baby gadoids suffer from the successive attacks of arrow worms, jellyfish, sea gooseberries and eventually of bigger fish such as cod, haddock, whiting and coalfish.

For many years we have realised that anglers, trawlermen and long-liners compete with the fish themselves to see who can catch the most. The amount of fish consumed by other fish is indeed very large. In fact, it is believed that the weight of fish eaten while still in the North Sea is on a par with that caught by all the fishing nations put together.

So big fish eat little fish, but, of course, it is much more complicated than that. Take just one example: using bigger mesh nets to conserve young cod also automatically reduces fishing pressure on smaller species such as

The good old days: Mike, in his late teens, poses with a cod caught on a heavy pirk and boat gear.

whiting. Thus protected, the numbers of whiting may then increase more quickly than those of cod and whiting eat a lot of baby cod, so fewer cod might make it to a size big enough to be trawled and turned into food. In this way, if not clearly understood and thought through carefully, protection measures could backfire and deplete stocks still further.

In 1991, to confirm their suspicions, Ministry scientists examined the stomachs of almost 35,000 fish taken from the North Sea. The prey of every single specimen were identified, counted and weighed. Extra information on how quickly food passes through the fish was also obtained. For example, it was found that tough foods such as shrimp take about five times as long to digest as a meal of soft fish or lugworm. Using this data the numbers of fish eaten each year can be calculated. The figures are complicated, but we already know that the late twentieth century crash in numbers of cod and their relatives was accompanied by an increase in populations of mid-water fish such as herring and sprat.

In addition to mere statistics, we can learn something from these studies about how to catch fish. For example, it provides a real insight into the main foods of the big cod that we seek. The stomachs may be half-full of crab, but if these tough customers stay undigested for, say, ten times as long as the fish which are eaten, it suggests that crabs are perhaps less attractive to the fish than they might appear.

If we want to catch bigger cod than average we might have to reconsider which baits to use in particular circumstances. 'So what!' you might say, 'I only bait with lug, crab, mussel or ragworm. I couldn't care less whether whiting eat cod or vice versa.' You should care. For a start, whether we like it or not, the quality of your fishing is greatly influenced by the knock-on effects of commercial fishing. If, perish the thought, the men from the ministry get it wrong there may be no cod, whiting or haddock for us to catch in future years. Our children and grandchildren may never see a codling bigger than 15 in and the long, cold waits between bites could be even longer than they are at present.

The modern ways: a cod which took a soft plastic fished on light, high-end Japanese lure fishing gear from his boat. Captor: Austen Goldsmith. Picture: Simon Everett.

Eat or be eaten

Whether on land or in the sea, predation is a fact of nature. We have all watched TV footage of hunting predators on the plains of Africa, the lion, the cheetah or the hyena singling out the young or weak specimen of its prey before catching and eating it. Things are no different for the fish around our shores. There is a constant struggle between hunters and hunted, large and small, weak and strong. Most of the fish that we like to catch are designed to prey on smaller animals and many of them eat other fish.

A couple of studies show just how tricky it is to be a cod. Fishery scientists like to study what they call 'habitat', which simply means the sort of places that fish choose to live in. It is well known that young, small fish often live in or around cover (hiding places) to give them a chance of dodging predators. To test this idea some Canadian researchers studied how baby cod managed to avoid the evil intentions of their older relatives. The experiment was carried out in tanks and the baby cod were given the choice of sand, gravel, big stones or a clump of kelp to hide in. Bigger, three-year-old cod were introduced to the tanks as predators.

If there was no big cod in the tank or if the big cod was in there but had decided to take a rest (no, they are not always on the prowl), the little cod preferred to swim about over the sandy seabed and avoided the kelp, at the same time keeping well clear of the predator. If, however, the big cod decided it was hungry and began to forage about the tank, everything changed and the little cod, sensing the danger, dived for cover. Surprisingly, given the choice, the baby fish hid among the big stones and the kelp was only regarded as a second-best refuge. When they were able to tuck themselves away in either stones or weed there was much less chance of being eaten.

Presumably hiding among and under stones gives these baby fish better protection than lurking among waving weeds and little cod are not the only ones to realise this. We have often seen young mullet and bass, which normally swim around in shoals, disappear like magic when they were disturbed. By searching about with our hands and turning over stones the refugees were often discovered neatly tucked away in crevices.

Some time ago there was a television programme in which several species of tropical fish were shown turning over large rocks to get at the animals hiding beneath, while other opportunist fish looked on. It would surprise us if some of our own predators, perhaps large cod or wrasse, do not use exactly the same tactics. In fact, cod are well-known stone turners.

From a very different point of view, another Canadian study was interested in just how much big cod move about when they are in the sea and how they shoal together. In this case, sensitive echo sounders were used to follow the yearly shoreward migration of cod shoals, which occurs every spring over the Newfoundland shelf. It was found that both the tightness of the shoals and the rate at which the cod swam were closely associated with the presence of pink shrimps in the water. These shrimps are those big succulent prawns you can buy at any fishmonger's. Even when dead and cooked, these juicy crustaceans are superb salmon baits and when they are alive and kicking they are an important food for cod and other fish.

The shrimp shoals show up on echo-sounding traces as background scatter so it was possible to tell where their numbers were thickest. The migrating cod, which were usually swimming towards the coast at a speed of about 14 miles per day, dropped their speed to about three miles per day when they encountered large numbers of shrimp. Presumably the wealth of food was just too much for them to resist and the fish got stuck in when they had the chance. Even the urge to migrate was overcome by the chance of a mega square meal.

In fact, cod do not spend the whole of their lives near the seabed, passing much of their time well up in the water. A second interesting observation by the Canadians was that the feeding cod shoals spread out from the seabed to match exactly the depth range of the shrimp hordes. This upward and outward spread meant that the cod were swimming in open water anything up to 85 yards off the bottom. The cod would not rise any further from the bottom than this, even if there were lots of shrimps at shallower depths.

When the cod were feeding on these big concentrations of shrimps the shoals actually dispersed to do so and at times the individual fish were as far as eight body lengths apart. This means that in a shoal of big fish, each, say, 3 ft long, the feeding individuals could be as much as 24 ft from one another. The scientists interpret these changes in swimming speed and shoal structure as ways of making the most of the rich food supply.

Why do cod shoal in this way? For any fish, being in a shoal probably gives them a number of advantages when it comes to avoiding predators. You might think that a fish swimming in a crowd would have more competition for food (less shrimps to go round), but at the same time it can feed more freely because there are more pairs of eyes (and in fish, other senses) on the lookout for danger. All in all, these snippets of information are simply more pieces in the great puzzle of what makes our favourite fried fish supper the great success it is.

A fine mid-winter cod. Probably a member of a widespread shoal. Captor: Rod Lugg. Picture: Austen Goldsmith.

The catch

Gliding through the waving fronds of a kelp forest the cod stopped at intervals to investigate a brittle star or a crab scuttling for cover. Along with its shoalmates it had been having a thin time, food was scarce in the cold northern waters, but spring, and a time of plenty, was just around the corner. As the big red-brown fish emerged from the cover of the weed onto the sandy seabed plain, a glint of silver caught its eye – whiting! Twisting and turning the cod shoal ripped, again and again, into the massed ranks of their smaller cousins.

Flash! Flash! Flash! The big cod glimpsed another easy meal and turned back from the haven of the kelp for a final snack. One sweep of its great tail took it within reach of the little darting fish and the huge coal scuttle of a mouth opened to engulf its victim. Carried by the inrush of water the silver-plated pirk jerked upwards and its hook sank home into the bony jaw of the fish.

Far above on the heaving deck of a small boat, a young angler felt the throbbing resistance on his line, the carbon rod curved in response and the long, hard haul began. It was five minutes or more before the 30-pounder was heaved aboard to a chorus of 'Oohs!' and 'Aahs!' from the excited charter party.

Isn't this just the stuff real angling memories are made of? Let's hope that the story remains a reality for future generations.

chapter_**04**

EELS AND LAMPREYS
ANCIENT FISH WITH MODERN PROBLEMS

The amazing eel

Bob and Mike cast out their long strips of herring and settled down to await the onset of dusk. Their carp rods were propped up on rests and the bale-arms of the large fixed-spool reels were open to allow the 10 lb nylon to spill freely off, should a fish move away with the bait.

They had laid a carpet of minced herrings on the firm muddy bottom and, at intervals, a globule of oil would pop up and spread shimmering, coloured discs on the surface of the calm water to show where it lay.

Mike's tackle was the first in action and the silver-paper indicator rustled against the butt ring as a good run developed. He picked up the rod and gently folded the bale-arm closed. The line tightened and he tensed in preparation for a strike that would set the 2/0 hook. In his excitement he must have applied a little too much pressure, because the nylon fell slack as his customer rejected the bait.

Within minutes Bob's line was streaking out and, being more composed than Mike, he hooked his fish and after a respectable tug of war, an eel of about 3 ft in length came writhing onto the shore. As darkness closed in, ten more eels of a similar size were hooked and landed.

This account describes a fishing session in an old limestone quarry many years ago, but eels are still a favourite species with us. Wrigglers are now much sought after by many sea anglers, especially match fishermen who value a good bag of silver eels as something to be proud of.

Because catching eels seems to be popular it is appropriate to say a few words about how they fit into the sea angling world. In these days of lavish television natural history programmes, most people must be familiar with the incredible life history of the European eel (*Anguilla anguilla L.*). To summarise, the adult eels breed in the depths of the western Atlantic and the tiny, transparent larvae (leptocephali) then drift on the transoceanic currents for three years towards the coast of Europe. As they reach the shores of Britain the larvae change their form to become tiny eels (elvers), which then disperse to their feeding grounds. Many continue their journey by entering estuaries and rivers and become the freshwater eels that, decades later, migrate back to the Sargasso Sea to spawn, but some take up residence along the coast where, as green or yellow eels (also known as 'snotties' by anglers because of their slimy coating), they will devour as much dead or living animal material as they can get hold of.

It is at this stage that eels first become of interest to the sea angler. Everyone who has collected bait along the seashore must have, at some time, turned over a weedy boulder to find a grey-green, slimy, vulcanised creature splashing in the shallow puddle beneath. These little eels made cracking good baits for bass and pollack. Used live they caused tangles, but, free-lined or spun, a freshly killed 'bootlace' was hard to beat (with the recent crash in eel numbers, this is no longer a viable option). On one occasion, while Mike was fishing with some pals from the rocks of the Donegal coast, natural eels out-fished artificials in a ratio of about three to one. The dead eels were simply hooked through their heads with a 4/0, cast out, allowed to sink to the tips of the kelp fronds and retrieved slowly. The big olive-bronze pollack just grabbed the eel and gulped it down in one swift lunge.

All of these small shoreline-living eels are males. Just as in the case of their bigger relative the conger, the female fish are much, much bigger than the males. Over most of the year the small male eels are the only ones that take sea anglers' baits. We have caught them when we were fishing for flounder in Poole Harbour, when we were legering for wrasse at Chapman's Pool and when we were beach casting with lug for the cod of Chesil Beach. In other words, just as in fresh water, they can be caught almost everywhere.

Female eels are much, much bigger than the males.

Eels living out their lives in salty water are relatively small and, because of this, the average size of those hooked by sea anglers is generally nothing to write home about. Any eel of more than a pound or so is quite a creditable catch. However, in the autumn when the heavy rains cause rivers to swell with flood water, eels which have often spent 20 or more years in fresh water, move down to the sea using streams and rivers as their watery highways. Eels that have grown big and fat on a diet of roach, perch, earthworms, insects and slaters are suddenly overwhelmed by the urge to migrate. The bottom-burrowing, drably camouflaged creature, adapted to nocturnal existence in the holes and crevices of a lake or riverbed, must now become an ocean-going fish.

Having been little more than an eating machine in the form of a powerful muscular body terminating in rat-trap jaws driven by a solid mass of jaw muscles (quite different from the jaw mechanism of most other fish species), the eel's hormones now switch on a gradual change, which over a couple of years will reduce the fish to little more than a tough sausage-skin full of eggs or sperm.

The early stages of the transformation are those that interest the sea angler. Little piggy eyes enlarge to become large, lustrous, light-collectors for deep sea work. The impermeable skin with its coating of waterproof slime now has to keep water in against the highly concentrated salt solution outside, which is trying to suck it dry. In open water the greenish-yellow combat uniform is of little use and is replaced by silvery, mirror-like sides. Many other species of fish that migrate to the open sea have a similar strategy; seagoing salmon and sea trout, for example, have a nickel-plated appearance.

In estuaries silver eels are the quarry of many sea anglers. As your legered lugworm rests on the grey mud it is often a toss-up whether it will be taken by a flounder, a bass or a silver eel.

Eel selection

Is there any way that you can select for eels and give yourself a better chance of catching them? Because these fish are not specialist feeders, they are likely to take worm or crab with the same enthusiasm they show for fish or mussel. Like many other species, eels may be preoccupied or have search images for particular foods and this is sufficient to explain an apparent preference for ragworm in one estuary or fish in another. The only method that we ever employed successfully to avoid bass and flounders while eel fishing was a technique described by John Garrad, the man who developed the use of baited spoons for flounder fishing.

While fishing from a small dinghy in the estuary of the River Frome in Dorset, just where it enters Poole harbour, we caught quite a few decent eels by drifting a 2 in baited spoon in the current as the boat was resting at anchor. A small barrel lead was fitted at the head of the spoon to get it down and it was simply lowered over the stern and allowed to tick slowly over in the current, just above the muddy bottom. On a fast-flowing ebb tide the eels will often take such a drifted spoon almost at the surface; otherwise it is best to fish near the bed. On a good tide half a dozen eels in the 1–2 lb range would not be an exceptional catch using this method.

To sum up, the common eel is a fish beyond price. Good eating in its own right, the eel is also a premier attraction for predators such as bass, pollack and even tope. Eels bite freely on a range of baits and can be caught by a variety of methods. At the end of the day, when it comes down to a fight, the tough old eel takes a bit of beating and we can recall, on several occasions, having been completely fooled by a large eel's excellent simulation of a big old bass.

On a fast-flowing ebb tide big eels will often take a baited spoon drifted almost at the surface.

But there is a problem

Sadly, European eel stocks have seen a dramatic decline of 70–95% in many areas. No one knows for sure what the causes may be, but the decline appears to have coincided with the accidental introduction and spread of the parasitic Japanese eel nematode *Anguillicola crassus*, a worm that infests the swim bladder of eels and is thought to render the adult eels incapable of making their marathon spawning migration. Severe infestations can cause the death of the host.

This alien parasite found its way from Japanese eels (*Anguilla japonica*), imported into Europe in the early 1980s, where it transferred to *A. anguilla* with relative ease. The irony is that *A. japonica* seems unaffected by the blood-sucking worm. Instead, the inscrutable Japanese swim bladder nematode has found a host in the European eel, which has no natural defence against its advances.

Cunningly, the parasite transfers from eel to eel by passing its larvae out of the infected eel's digestive system, where they settle in the bottom sediment. The larvae are then eaten by a range of intermediate hosts – crayfish, copepods and small fish. Although eaten, they are not digested and set up temporary home, doing their landlord host no harm. When, in turn, their temporary accommodation is eaten by the eel, the transfer is completed.

Investigators studying European eels in Turkey have found infestation levels to be as high as 82%. A 1993 study, conducted in the Thames catchment by Pitcher and Moore, found parasitic nematode levels to be 12–32%. Given that other studies showed that *Anguillicola* has the ability to colonise and spread rapidly (in some cases, infestations have been recorded to rise from 10% to 50% in a year), it would be optimistic to suggest that the Thames eels are safe from the onward march of this invading threat.

It is not that no one knows of the plight of the European eel. Despite warnings from EU scientific advisers as far back as 2001, that the European eel fisheries are unsustainable and that eels are outside of 'safe biological limits' (a term used to suggest that fishing should be halted or restricted) the fishing of elvers (mostly for the Continental and Asian markets) continues to hamper the natural replenishment of eel stocks.

In 2008, on Somerset's River Parrett alone, 200 licences were granted to elver catchers, with 10 tons of elvers and glass eels being exported from the UK that year. Yet, here in England, it is anglers and anglers alone who in 2010 have been banned from retaining eels, while the commercial catches continue more or less unabated.

> The further upstream an eel migrates the more likely it is to become a big fat female.

Water abstraction, the construction of impassable river barriers and the loss of wetland habitats may have impeded eel migrations and restricted dispersal, while some even believe that climate change has caused a shift in the speed and direction of the Gulf Stream, disrupting the cycle of the eels' spawning migrations.

With the European eel up against it on so many fronts, is it any wonder that catches may be less frequent than in years gone by? We should treat eels, whatever their size, with respect and, whenever possible, they should be released to continue their time-honoured journeys.

Large eels migrate downstream in the autumn after as many as 20 years in fresh water.

CONGER: THE NOCTURNAL FISH EATER

So much for freshwater eels, but what do we know about their marine relative, the conger, that might help us in our attempts to catch them? There has been pathetically little research on these great eels, but perhaps the most useful information relates to what they eat.

Scientists Moriarty, O'Sullivan and Davenport made a study of conger diet, using 213 specimens caught from Irish waters in depths of up to 200 m. The fish were caught over a whole year and about half of them came from offshore. Almost all their prey consisted of fish, with whiting being the main victims inshore and blue whiting (an abundant deep water relative of the whiting) offshore. Crabs, squat lobsters, squid, cuttlefish and octopus were all found in stomachs, but were only a very small proportion of the diet.

A Spanish research team looked at the role of squid and octopus as food for the bottom-living species of fish in the southern Bay of Biscay during the autumn months. In this case, huge numbers of fish stomachs were examined (almost 43,000 stomach contents of 27 bottom-living fish species were analysed). These species represent the community of fish living in the southern Bay of Biscay. Overall, less than 1% of the food eaten by fish consisted of various squids, both small and large.

Congers were included in this survey and two-thirds of the conger caught had full stomachs. Very few had coughed up their stomach contents as they were landed so the results were pretty reliable. Only about 2% of their food consisted of squid. Bear in mind though that just because a predator does not eat squid it does not mean that it does not like it. The simple truth might be that it is just unable to catch it.

The North American conger (*Conger oceanicus*), which is very similar to our own conger eel (*Conger conger*), has also received some scientific attention. Just like the eels round the coasts of the UK, it was found that their American cousins mainly ate fish and crustaceans, with the bigger predators concentrating chiefly on other fish. The presence of a nocturnal eel-like fish, *Lepophidium*, in conger guts confirmed that congers are mainly nocturnal feeders (as we sea anglers know).

The conger eel is a widely distributed coastal fish that lives in a range of water depths. In the Azores there is an important, deepwater long-line fishery for conger. This fishery grew quickly in the 1980s, but the catch rates have declined in recent years (no doubt through over-fishing). The conger is one of the main species caught by the long-line fleet in coastal waters and on offshore banks. From 1981 to 1994 conger represented 13% of the total landings of these long-line fisheries in the Azores. During this period, landings of eels increased by about 400%.

A 20-something, 5 ft 8 in Mike with a shore-caught conger of about the same size.

Conger eels are bottom-swimming fish usually found on hard and sandy bottoms near rocks down to more than 180 m depth. In the Azores the conger eel is equally abundant in coastal areas and down to 55–110 m depth. They are active at night and tend to hide among rocks during the day. The conger may be very sensitive to exploitation because, like its freshwater cousins, it probably reproduces only once in its lifetime. The biology of the conger eel is being studied at present, but information is not yet available.

Again in the Azores more than 200 conger were caught during a wider research programme using long-lines which was aimed at studying bottom-living fishes. The work was carried out between March and May in both coastal areas and offshore banks. The long-line used in the experiments had hooks (Mustad 2335) tied on 15 in droppers one yard apart and baited with pieces of salted sardine. Line setting began before sunrise (about 05:00) and hauling started two hours later.

By grouping conger into four size classes between 2 ft and 6 ft in length it was possible to see whether there were any changes in diet as the fish got bigger. Of the 215 conger eels examined:

- 74 (34.4%) had empty stomachs.
- 22 (10.2%) had eaten only the salted sardine bait.
- 24 (11.2%) had eaten hooked fish caught on the long-line baits.
- Only 95 individuals (44.2%) had stomachs with 'proper food' not associated with the baited long-line.

The low number of full stomachs may be due to several reasons. The fact that the long-line is a passive fishing method suggests that well-fed fish are not so keen to take salted sardines (would you be?). Another reason is the occurrence of inside-out stomachs caused by the expansion of the swim bladder when a fish is brought to surface. Coughing up of stomach contents, caused by stress, may also occur. This fishing method itself could influence the quality of the food in the gut as hauling the line can take several hours and in this time the contents may become completely digested and non-identifiable. The long-line is also size-selective, which might explain the lack of small conger in the sample.

Conger are largely nocturnal.

From the fish sampled, total length was measured. Recognition of sex and maturity of conger eel is very tricky and was not done. Fish that obviously had eaten hooked fish on the long-line were ignored. Frequency of occurrence, percentage numbers and weight were noted. For diet comparisons, prey species were grouped. Prey that occurred rarely were lumped together and called 'others'.

The stomachs of these 95 'naturally feeding' conger eels were opened up to see what they had been eating. All in all, from these conger eel stomachs, 215 prey were identified, belonging to about 17 different types. As in the other studies it was concluded that conger eel feed almost exclusively on fish, which occurred in 95% of stomachs, accounted for 99% of total contents by weight and made up 97% of all food items counted. Other prey types, including crabs, squids and so on, contributed little to the overall diet.

Fish are the main prey of conger. Around our coasts whiting are one of the chief victims.

By far the most common fish eaten were red band fish (a burrowing, eel-like fish) and snipefish (a 6 in long nocturnal plankton feeder). Both these species of prey fish are active only in the hours of darkness.

Interestingly, prey composition shows that although conger mainly forage near the seabed on bottom-living prey they can feed higher in the water column on mid-water species if they have to. Conger ate quite a number of free-swimming fishes, such as mackerel and scad (don't ask us how they catch them). However, all sizes of conger eels mainly concentrated on the two favoured species. So once again conger ate lots of fish. There were no obvious differences in diet between fish of different sexes or between big conger and small conger.

The conger eel (unlike its freshwater cousin) seems to be specialised to prey upon fish. The dominance of fishes in the diet of conger eel was also reported from the shores of Spain, for conger of more than 14 in long, and from the central eastern Mediterranean. Again, most of the species consumed by this predator live on or near the seabed. Wherever they occur, conger are always noted for their nocturnal activity pattern. It has been reported that the relative importance of crabs and squat lobsters is greater in the diet of conger eel smaller than 14 in, but who wants to catch them? We suggest that you stick to your fish baits and hold out for a biggie.

LAMPREYS

Mike's wife, Lilian, is a Geordie and the daughter of a trawler skipper. Some of her relations still live in the town of North Shields at the mouth of the River Tyne. For 15 years Mike also lived and did most of his fishing in that area. Much of the boat fishing in northeast England is for cod and codling. The tackle has probably changed a bit these days, but it used to be traditional northeast coast boat gear designed for hauling fish out of kelpy, rough ground.

The rods were, to say the least, stout and the reels were often home-made, large diameter 'Scarborough' type centrepins with very thick line.

We have no intention of discussing the rights and wrongs of different sorts of tackle, but a conversation that Mike had with one of his in-laws (also a keen angler) last time he was up there stuck in his mind. They were talking about the pleasures of catching codling when it was recalled that among the other species that 'Cousin John' caught on the same tackle were lampreys. He said that when lampreys appeared on the scene other fish vanished.

Now we are talking second-hand information here, so it would not be wise for us to speculate too far. We are not sure what sort of lampreys John was talking about nor even that by 'lamprey' he meant the same thing as us. It seems likely, but we have been caught out by local names before. However, we wondered if anyone else had caught them on bait or encountered them in the course of fishing for other species.

Our own encounters with lampreys have been of a different nature. Some years ago, when it was legal, we used to catch small eels for bass baits. The technique was simply to swish a pond net through the mud and weeds of a little local river and then pick through the contents of the net for eels. We found that many of the eel-like creatures trapped in the bag of our nets were not *Anguilla anguilla* at all but muscular, greeny-brown, pencil-like animals with sucker mouths and tiny eyes. Along each side of what passed for a neck, just where the single gill opening of an eel should be, were neat rows of little holes (hence the local name 'nine eyes').

These were the larvae (ammocoetes) of brook lampreys, curious little creatures which spend several years sifting microscopic algae from the riverbed mud before changing into mature adult brook lampreys. These adults are silver-skinned actively swimming wrigglers with more than a passing resemblance to marine sandeels. The sole function of the mature specimens is to dig a shallow nest in the gravel of the riverbed where they can lay their eggs.

Why should a fish, which spends its entire life in or on the bed of a river, be of any interest to sea anglers? Apart from their value as baits (they are protected nowadays, of which more later), our other species of lamprey spend a good deal of their lives in the sea. They are, in fact, parasites of other fish. Having passed their juvenile stages in riverbed mud feeding on algae and detritus they transform into the vampires of the fish world.

The river lamprey looks exactly like the bigger version of the brook lamprey, but at the end of its mud-burrowing larval stage it dons a silver skin and heads down to the sea. River lampreys do not go far from the estuary. They fatten up and develop their eggs and sperm on a rich diet of estuarine fish and migrants such as sea trout and shad. Around the mouth is a sucker-like disc by which the parasite clings tenaciously to its unfortunate hosts. Within the sucker a set of sharp teeth assists clinging and other teeth, on the tongue, rasp a hole in the skin through which the lamprey extracts the blood and body fluids of the fish. Enzymes in the lamprey's saliva dissolve the tissues of the host and this 'soup' is also sucked up.

The largest of our lampreys is the sea lamprey, which can be three feet long and as thick as your arm. Like the other lamprey species, the larvae live in the river mud, but the adults are sea fish with a skin the colour of a camouflaged combat jacket. Victims of the sea lamprey include a wide range of popular fish such as cod, haddock, coalfish and pollack. Salmon are also attacked and, to add insult to injury, the sea lamprey spawns on the same river gravel as the salmon, by excavating a great crater in which to lay its eggs. The sucker mouth is brought into play for nest building. Lumps of gravel, stones and cobbles are picked up and carted out of the nesting area to be dumped round its edge. The adults then die after spawning.

To return to lampreys as sea baits, we used to fish with them in two different situations. Swanage beach boasts a long, golden sandy strand. At the eastern end are a series of low wooden groynes designed to reduce longshore movement of the sand. When the wind blows from an easterly quarter the surf pounds sand into suspension and, as the tide floods, bass work along the sea's edge, picking up small creatures disturbed by the wave action. A legered bait cast into the boiling sea stands a pretty good chance of attracting bass. Young lampreys seemed to be better baits than many for this purpose. In fact, it did not seem to make much difference whether the bait was a brown ammocoete larva or a silvery adult, the schoolies gobbled them up as fast as they could.

Two of our lamprey species migrate to sea and are parasitic on fish.

The other place where we used brook lampreys for bait was from the old Ferry Bridge on the Portland to Weymouth causeway. Adult lampreys were collected in a pond net from their communal spawning areas and fished as livebaits on a flowing trace and size 6 hook. As at Swanage, there were very few large bass about so early in the season, but pollack and schoolies took the lampreys as keenly as they devoured any sandeel. In those days, of course, the lamprey was not an endangered species.

As mentioned, lampreys are now protected, so using them as baits is no longer an option, but they are still likely to be on the radar of bass and pollack. There are several new soft plastic lures which, although intended to resemble

Eels are in trouble and the causes are complex and varied, but mostly man-made.

sandeels, bear more than a passing likeness to small lampreys and we see no reason why these should not attract the attention of the predators.

Neither of us has ever caught a lamprey while angling, although we have heard of them taking legered worms in rivers. We are still curious to hear of experiences similar to those recounted by John. Does the presence of lampreys really put fish off the feed? Are the many species of fish which play host to these parasitic hangers-on frightened off by the prospect of picking up a blood-sucking hitch-hiker? This does not seem to fit in with their obvious value as bait, but stranger things have happened.

HAGFISH

There is a little-known close relative of the lamprey that sea anglers may encounter from time to time.

In his youth Mike used to spend quite a lot of time catching fish off the coast of Northumberland. He enjoyed any sort of fishing, from dropping a limpet-baited line into rock pools for crabs or blennies, to hand-lining from small boats for codling and coalfish, or going out with the ring netters to catch herrings. It can be just as exciting to watch the net rising to the surface, with thousands of herring splashing and flashing within the headline, as feeling a bite or seeing the float dip. Occasionally, under the yellow glow of the lights, a big predatory fish, such as a monkfish, would be seen ploughing through the mass of herring in the net.

One of his most memorable experiences happened during a potting trip in a coble from Seahouses. They were up at the crack of dawn to lift the pots. The sea was calm and there was only a slight breeze. Mike hooked the pot buoy into the boat and with a couple of turns of rope around the winch began to haul. The crabs and lobsters were removed and the pots rebaited as they came aboard, with carcasses of coalfish caught the day before.

One or two of the creels were empty, but it was a good haul and most contained one or more hefty crustaceans. As Mike leaned forward to lift the last one he noticed that there was a fish inside. It was not just the remains of the bait but a sizeable codling that must have had trouble squeezing through the entrance. A closer look showed that the cod was stone dead – quite surprising since the pots had been set only a day before. Mike unlaced the pot and took hold of the fish to remove it. As he did so, a squirming, eel-like shape emerged from its belly and fell onto the boards – shades of the film *Alien*. The skipper leaned over, dipped up a bucket of seawater, picked up the writhing fish and dropped it in. Within minutes the water in the container seemed to thicken before their eyes until it resembled wallpaper paste – it was quite incredible.

Mike had encountered eel slime before, but never anything like this. The animal was only about 15 in long and yet it had filled the whole bucket with slime. Mike's friends told him that this was a hagfish or slime eel. He had heard of these creatures, but this was the first time he had ever seen one and he had assumed that they were quite rare. Recent studies, however, seem to tell a different story.

Firstly, what are hagfish? They have been called 'living fossils'. The oldest known specimens are found in rocks 330 million years old and if they were alive would be quite recognisable today. The fish are smooth and eel-shaped with only one small fin that extends around the tail end. They are so flexible that they can (and do) tie themselves in a reef knot.

The mouth is quite small and lies in a groove, surrounded by short tentacles, underneath the head. Inside the mouth two sharp plates and a set of prickly 'thorns' take the place of jaws. By flapping the plates the slime eel can hack its way into the bodies of injured or dying fish. They find it difficult to bite through skin or scales so they generally attack by entering the gills, mouth or other openings. The hagfish have no real eyes (although some fossil species had large eyes).

Hagfish can be a real curse to fishermen setting long-lines because many of the hooked fish may be totally eaten, from the inside out, before the lines are lifted. It used to be thought that these relatives of the lamprey were quite scarce, but it is now known that there are more than 60 species. They are so common in some parts of the world that they form the basis of extensive commercial fisheries. American scientists have estimated that in certain areas well over a million hagfish are present on every square mile of seabed.

As other fish populations have declined, hags are now being caught in huge numbers, mainly for their skins. The skins can be tanned and turned into smooth, high-quality leather. The leather then finds its way into designer goods including handbags, purses, briefcases and even shoes. In the first five years (up to 1996) of fishing a newly discovered hotspot off the North American Atlantic coast, more than 50 million slime eels were caught and processed.

The method used to catch these eyeless, ghoulish animals is simple. Plastic barrels, drilled with small holes for entry and baited with fish scraps, are lowered to the sea bed. The fish slither into the barrels after the food and become trapped by their own slime. In good fishing spots as many as 100 fish have been known to enter a trap in the first hour after it was set. Unfortunately, hagfish grow slowly and only lay a few eggs at a time so they quickly become over-fished. Already the numbers caught per trap and the size of the fish taken are decreasing in some key fisheries.

What about the main feature of these animals, the incredible slime? It is produced from several hundred special glands along the body. Normally this mucus eases the passage of the hag into its prey. When they are disturbed or threatened, however, they really go to town and a single fish can easily produce a bucketful of slimy gunge within a few minutes. A sticky whitish liquid oozes from the skin of the fish and rapidly swells to several hundred times its own volume. Eel fishermen do not know the meaning of 'snotty' unless they have seen a hagfish.

Since hagfish eat all sorts of carrion (as well as living fish) and can be abundant, it is likely that, from time to time, one will be hooked and landed by an angler. If you should be the lucky(?) person, treat your catch with respect – its ancestry is a lot longer than yours, by more than 300 million years.

chapter_05

FLATFISH
WONDERS OF THE
UNDERSEA WORLD

First flatties

One of the trickiest tasks facing any sea angler can be introducing the kids to fishing. Our own children when they were young were always keen to 'have a cast', but they were soon bored if no bites were forthcoming. It is therefore essential to make sure that newcomers to the sport, young or old, have a good chance of catching something. There is no point in long boring campaigns to catch specimen fish or sophisticated methods that need weeks to perfect. Lots of bites and a few fish, however small and insignificant, are the order of the day when you are new to the sport – it is how we got hooked.

From November onwards the tidal reaches of our local rivers seethe with flounders, from postage stamp size upwards, and these fish (the bigger ones at any rate) provide a perfect training ground for the up-and-coming sea angler. By casting ragworm on light leger gear five or ten yards out you can almost guarantee that within minutes the rod top will rattle to the pull of a flatty. A quick strike to make sure that the hook is not buried deep inside the fish (small circle hooks might help) and the line will sheer to and fro as another hand-sized specimen is reeled to the shore. Whether the sun is blazing down, the river is high in a dirty flood or there are hordes of Sunday dog walkers or cyclists passing to and fro along the riverside path, the flounders can be relied upon to co-operate.

Having introduced flatfish as easy catches or 'fish for kids', it would be wrong to suppose that these curious creatures are somehow inferior. The flounder and its relatives belong to one of the most highly evolved and sophisticated groups of fish in the world. They are adapted to swimming on one side, their eyes and mouth are twisted to fit their odd shape and their search-and-destroy feeding equipment would rival anything designed by modern military engineers.

Plaice and sole senses

Many people find the various types of flatfish confusing. This is hardly surprising because they are all shaped and camouflaged to skim along, unseen, on the seabed. The senses of feeling, taste, smell and sight are those that feature most strongly in the flatty's armoury. All flatfish have two eyes on the upper surface and two 'noses', a small one on the blind side and a bigger one on top.

Take plaice and sole, for example: both eat worms, shrimps and cockles of various sorts, but the sole feeds mostly at night and is believed to use its senses of touch, smell and taste, while the plaice is a daylight feeder using both sight and smell to locate its prey. The sole has big nostrils on its snout and lots of fine whiskery papillae on the underside of its head. It used to be thought that the whiskers were simply tasting organs, but more recent research has suggested that they are, in fact, associated with touch receptors (feelers) and help the fish to feel for its prey (presumably as well as tasting it).

Clive Hodges displays his 3 lb 4 oz sole. Note the black spot on the pectoral fin and the rippling marginal fins with which the sole creeps along the seabed. Picture: Mike Harding.

The plaice is a dedicated sight feeder and responds to visual attractors.
Picture: Chris Guest.

The Dover sole is a master of nocturnal hunting. Creeping about the seabed in the hours of darkness or when storms have turned the water the colour of oxtail soup, these bloodhounds of the undersea world have no trouble finding the tiniest morsel of worm on the blackest night. How do they do that?

Experiments in the Netherlands have shown that the sole sniffs out prey which is lying quite still on the seabed by using the nostrils on its eyed topside. If these are plugged to prevent the flow of water to the nose, the fish has great difficulty locating prey. However, the sole has another trick up its sleeve. The furry touch sensors on the blind side of the head also allow the fish to feel for its prey on the sea floor. Recent studies have shown that the nocturnal sole has ten times as many smell sensors in its nose as the daytime-feeding plaice and three times the area of smelling tissue. No wonder sole will ignore food dangling directly above their heads as they search the surface of the sand for shrimps.

The plaice depends much more on its eyes to locate prey. Smelling and tasting food is a lot less important to the plaice than the sole. Even the section of the brain used for smelling food is a great deal smaller in the plaice than in the sole and the reverse is true of the section concerned with vision – hence the apparent benefit of beads and spoons as visual attractors for plaice. Flounder and other similar daylight-active species are probably equipped in much the same way as their red-spotted relative.

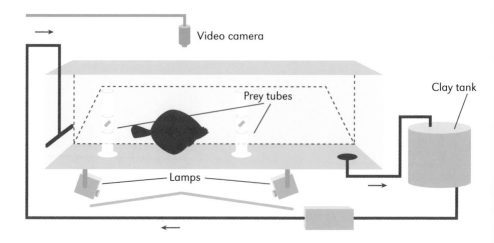

Tank used to test the importance of sight and smell to hunting fish. Clay particles can be added to colour the water.

By comparing the behaviours of sole and plaice, Batty and Hoyt have been able to separate the importance of touch and taste/smell for feeding in these fish. For the experiment the flatfish were observed in the dark, using sensitive video cameras and infra-red light, and they were offered little shrimp-like animals as food. The scientists used special chemicals, which temporarily numb particular senses, to find out exactly how flatfish locate their food in daylight and in darkness. The 'feel' receptors, for example, could be knocked out with an antibiotic to see how the fish managed without their sense of touch. Both plaice and sole were able to feed, day and night. However, when the sense of touch had been numbed, sole had difficulty catching live prey, but were still able to find dead food.

To cut a long story short, it seems that the sole were almost as happy without their touch receptors but plaice, with or without them, were not much good at finding dead prey in the dark. As suggested, sole do use touch to find live (moving) prey but depend mainly on taste/smell to discover food. Plaice, on the other hand, require both vision and taste/smell to hunt effectively. Both species swing their heads from side to side when searching in the dark. Sole often overshoot dead prey before going into reverse to pick it up and probably tasting the food before eating it. Plaice, in contrast, usually take such food into the mouth (if they manage to find it) and, should it be found wanting, they spit it (and your hook) out again.

Sole find food mainly by touch and scent. Plaice find food mainly by sight.

These observations agree with previous work conducted in the Netherlands. Sole are just as successful when feeding at night-time or in dirty water as in daylight, although they are much more active in the dark. Plaice, on the other hand, feed mainly in the daytime and find their prey by sight. They do, however, use their sense of smell (but not their sense of touch) and will continue to feed, although to a much lesser extent, at night.

Where does this leave us when it comes to increasing our catches of flatfish? Clearly, if we want to be selective, we must fish for sole in the dark (or in very dirty water) and there is probably no need to move the bait about – the fish will search it out. They must also be allowed plenty of time to taste it and pick it up. Plaice will take better in daylight and we should use every possible strategy of shape, colour, size and movement to draw their attention to the bait. Nothing new in any of this really, but at least it shows that the existing approaches of experienced sea anglers are along the right lines.

Colour change

On a slightly different tack, most anglers are aware that flatfish come in right-eyed (such as sole and plaice) and left-eyed (such as turbot and brill) varieties.

> Some flatfish can change colour to match the background accurately in just a few seconds.

The side that has the eyes develops camouflage colours, allowing the fish to escape predators or to hide on the seabed while they are hunting. In the past it has been suggested that certain flatfish were able to improve their camouflage by imitating their surroundings. For example, some experiments as far back as 1911 seemed to show that a flatfish could change colour, over a period of days, to copy a chessboard pattern. More recent studies suggested that this work was wrong and concluded that the results were due partly to photographic problems.

Just a few years ago, scientists in California set out to answer the question once and for all. They showed that not only could flatties blend into the background with ease but they could also mimic checkerboard patterns in a flash (2–8 seconds), a speed that would put the famed chameleon to shame. Tropical flatfish were much better at this colour change than our own cold-water species. They were even able to copy big polka dot patterns by producing two large dark spots on the skin. The precision and fantastic speed of these changes suggest that the fish sees the pattern and its brain instantly signals the message to the pigment cells (chromatophores) in the skin – a trick that, as far as we know, no other animals (except possibly some squid and octopus) are able to do.

Next time you are down at the coast and your mate reels in a flounder, dab or plaice don't say 'it's only another small flatty' and rip it off the hook. Handle it carefully, like the marvel that it is, and return it to the sea to grow bigger and fight another day.

How far should you cast?

Is it worth casting a long way when you are flatty fishing? Yes, at times. The benefits of a good casting range are most likely to be apparent when trying to target your bait on a particular species, like plaice. We should explain that a long cast is most likely to produce the biggest specimens because of the well-established connection between depth of water and size of plaice. Over gently shelving sand the deepest water is almost always furthest from the water's edge and that is where the expert will seek his match winner or frying-pan filler.

These fish almost always swim over relatively sandy ground in search of their prey, which is mostly molluscs such as cockles and clams, so the shore angler will usually find himself propelling his chosen bait over areas of nice, clean seabed. There is no problem about using fine lines and appropriate shock leaders to gain extra distance because the haunts of these flatties tend to be more or less snag-free. Longer casts can be achieved with relatively fine lines and luckily, although plaice are powerful muscular creatures, they are only about the size of a freshwater chub so hefty tackle is not necessary to subdue them.

The fact that small plaice tend to spend their time in shallower water than their elders and betters does not mean that they stay at one level all the time. Between the tide marks, on some stretches of coast, the water may change from zero to 40 ft deep in the space of only six hours and if the fish are to find their preferred depth of water they must move in and out with the ebb and flow.

Dr Gibson, a scientist of the Scottish Marine Biological Association, has spent many hours plaice watching. Gibson's idea was to find out how these popular flatfish behaved in relation to the rising and falling of the sea. He anchored his small rubber dinghy in shallow water so that it could be easily moved to any fixed point. The fish were observed through a large glass-bottomed bucket. By watching individual fish (nearly 400 of them in all) and making careful notes of how they moved and the direction in which they were headed it was possible to build up a picture of general patterns of behaviour.

The swimming movements of the plaice were of two types: firstly there were the longer periods of activity, lasting for more than a second. These seemed to be designed simply for getting from A to B as quickly as possible. Secondly, there were short bursts lasting for only a fraction of a second that the fish used when it was actively searching for food.

The limitations of visibility meant that observations were confined to shallow water (up to 7–8 ft) and to fairly young/small fish, but there is no reason to think that the big fish behave very differently. As you might expect, the fish moved up the shore on the flood tide. This movement took place over quite a short period, when the water was about 3 ft or 4 ft deep, and began about two hours after low water. During this inshore movement most of the swimming was of the brief, food-searching type (so the fish were feeding).

On the ebb, roughly two hours before low water, the fish shifted back down the shore. This time the movements were much more purposeful and involved little feeding activity. No wonder then that catches of these flatfish are generally better on the incoming tide.

Feeding facts

While on the subject of flatfish and scientific studies, it may be worth taking a look at some recent observations on their food and feeding. Unfortunately, most of the work was carried out in

Plaice feed actively as they move inshore on the flood tide.

North America or New Zealand so the species were different from those that we fish for. However, the principles are exactly the same and we will try to translate the results to our familiar species.

The first thing of note is that, despite their apparent similarity in appearance, flatfish species are not randomly scattered on the seabed. Fish eaters such as the brill and turbot are normally to be found on areas of coarse sediment where tidal currents are stronger and the prey (usually other fish) are most vulnerable to their lurking attacks. Dabs will be found over sand where shrimps and beach fleas are common, plaice concentrate in areas rich in mussels or cockles, while flounders will often hunt for crabs, worms and molluscs in estuaries where mud is the main type of sediment. Although there is a certain amount of overlap in the diets of the different kinds of fish, each is an expert when it comes to catching its own preferred 'niche' food.

Sometimes pollution, silting, dredging or spoil dumping has the effect of changing large areas of the seabed into an absolutely uniform, desert-like plain. Such areas often provide a very monotonous diet of only one or two species of worms for the resident flatties and the numbers and size of the fish suffer accordingly.

Research has turned up some useful and interesting facts about the feeding of flatfish. The first thing we found was an old study from the 1960s by a Dutch scientist called de Groot. He was interested in the way that different types of flatfish are adapted to catching and eating different prey. He started off by examining the guts and the gill rakers of a whole range of species. Turbot and brill, which eat large prey such as sandeels and other fish, have big mouths with sharp, inwardly curving teeth and strongly toothed gill rakers to prevent escape of the wriggling victims. Fish is fairly easy to digest so their guts are short and pretty simple.

Flounder, dab and plaice all have similar guts (a bit more complicated than those of the out-and-out fish eaters) because they all tend to feed on the same sort of animals (worms, shrimps and cockles), but notice that the slightly more predatory flounder has stronger teeth on the gill rakers than the others.

The flounder and dab have blunt, conical teeth in the mouth adapted to the capture of shrimps and other crustaceans, while the plaice has chisel-like teeth in the lower (blind side) jaw that it uses for biting bits off the siphons of clams and cockles. Whereas flounders have conical, all-purpose throat teeth, plaice have crushing molars that seem tailor-made for breaking up the shells of molluscs. The twisted, undershot mouth of the sole is clearly adapted for sucking in worms. Its gill rakers are almost smooth and the gut is a long and winding tube.

All this complicated anatomical stuff tells us quite a bit about the probable best baits to use for these species. Studies on sense organs and behaviour can

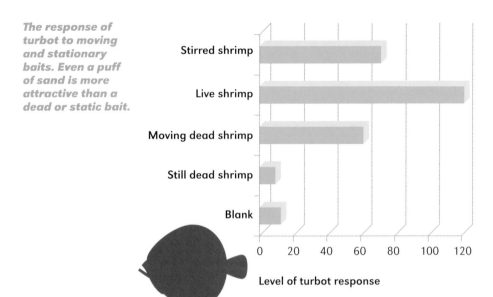

The response of turbot to moving and stationary baits. Even a puff of sand is more attractive than a dead or static bait.

The turbot, a lurking predator and a sucker for a moving bait, is perfectly camouflaged for its shell gravel habitat. Captor: Clive Hodges. Picture: Kim Hodges.

This time, a brill. A close relative of the turbot, the brill is smaller and more oval in shape but has similar habits. Captor: Clive Hodges. Picture: Kim Hodges.

add to this. As you might expect, turbot and brill feed largely by sight and are active only in daylight. Plaice, flounder and dab are also mainly daytime feeders and use their eyes to guide them to prey. However, all three have a well-developed sense of smell/taste and in the presence of prey-scent will search for it more actively than if there is no smell in the water. The sole is an out-and-out lover of darkness with extremely well-developed scent/taste systems and a very touch-sensitive underside – both useful for finding food in the dark or in coloured water.

Turn-ons for turbot

To return to turbot: smaller turbot eat a lot of shrimps and these were the food offered in tests carried out by scientists Holmes and Gibson. The shrimps used were about a quarter of the fish length. The prey were placed on the end of little thin glass rods and presented to the turbot either moving or still, live or dead. The shrimps could be moved smoothly or jerked. The responses of the turbot to the different bait presentations were scored: 0 for totally ignored up to 5 for a full-out attack on the bait. It is believed that turbot prefer their prey to be long and skinny, about eight times (five to ten times) as long as deep, and to be moving. It was noticed that turbot showed interest when the sand was disturbed so this was another factor in the study. Motionless shrimps or blank glass tubes were of no interest at all to the fish. Moving dead shrimps and sand disturbed by a glass rod certainly had an appeal for the turbot, but moving, live shrimps were far and away the best.

Moving livebaits are by far the best attractors for turbot.

In the other experiments it was found that the kicking legs of a living shrimp were an additional attraction. Long, thin prey animals were also of importance. Attempts to make an artificial shrimp were worthwhile, but, although slightly better than poorer copies, fiddling about to produce an exact imitation of a shrimp (with eyes, head, tail and a counter-shaded body) was really a waste of time.

Flounder: jack of all trades

Over the years a good deal has been learned about the behaviour of flounders. Some of this is common knowledge and some is not. Apart from the fact that the fish swim into almost unbelievably shallow water as the tide makes, it also became obvious from the pattern of catches that they move in shoals, which are often composed of similar-sized fish. Several such waves of fish will pass by your fishing position on a single tide. The presence of a hooked fish (a flounder or, for that matter, any other fish) on one of the three traces (of a three-hook flapper rig, for example) will, if left for a short time, usually attract a flounder to one of the other baits. Flounders often take fish baits as well as the usual king rag or crab.

Perhaps the most important lesson was one that will surprise most people. Despite the crude and heavy nature of the tackle we used in years gone by (originally a flax hand-line with a 3 or 4 oz weight), the fact that the line was held, at all times, between finger and thumb, allowed accurate judgment of what was going on beneath the water surface. The rattling tug of a 6 in coalfish was quite distinct from the heavy pull of a two-pounder or the dragging bite of a flounder. Even more important from the line-fisher's point of view was the way in which it was possible to judge the precise instant when the fish had taken the bait firmly into its mouth and could be struck and hooked with confidence.

A sharp lift of the wrist and forearm, at the correct moment, almost invariably resulted in a hooked fish. The proportion of missed bites was less than in almost any method we have encountered since and certainly far superior to that enjoyed by anglers accustomed to using rested rods. Some of these observations fell into place in later years and much of the following is based on the way in which our knowledge of flatties subsequently developed.

The flounder is quite often found over the same ground as its relative the plaice, although the latter is chiefly a fish of the open sea. As Dr. Michael Kennedy points out in his book *The Sea Angler's Fishes*, the flounder is much more of a fish eater than its red-spotted cousin. Sandeels, gobies, herring fry and, in fresh water, minnows and elvers are all mentioned as items of flounder diet. Our own experiences bear this out and include a 3.5 lb fish taken on live sandeel from a sandy-bottomed estuary, many large specimens caught on bottom-fished herring strips and several modest flounders of a pound or less which engulfed legered live minnows intended for trout or sea trout in the lower (freshwater) reaches of Dorset rivers.

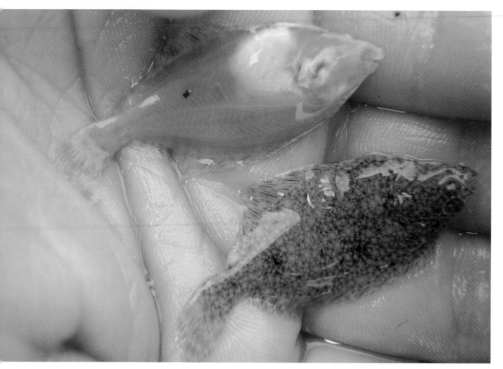

Baby flounders: only the size of postage stamps but already perfectly formed.

Perhaps the most interesting aspect of the flounders' fish-eating tendencies is the way in which they will attack not only real fish but also artificial baits. On holiday in Donegal with three pals many years ago, Mike fished the estuary of the little River Owenea where it wandered across a broad stretch of muddy sand to the Atlantic Ocean. At one point the river widened out into a good-sized pool that almost seemed to be paved with flounders. They caught quite a few fish on light-legered lugworm and clam. Mike added a white plastic luggage label, from his suitcase, to his trace as an attractor but caught no more fish than any of his mates, presumably because there were such a lot of flatties present that the bait was always within view of one or more.

As the tide began to flood into the pool one of the lads landed a sea trout of about 2 lb on worm and this prompted Mike to switch to spinning in the hope of catching another. The leger tackle was removed from the 6 lb line and replaced by a size two 'Mepps Mino', which is a spinning blade followed by a soft rubber fish, armed with a double hook and a small tail treble. The result of the experiment was not the expected trout but a whole series of hefty flounders, each with the rubber minnow well in its mouth. Interestingly, and in total contrast, in John Garrad's extensive experiments with the baited spoon he tried many comparisons between baited and unbaited lures of all kinds. The results show that he never caught a flounder on the artificials unless they were adorned with bait, preferably ragworm.

We are sure that many anglers must have taken odd flounders on artificials and some have even taken flounders on fly gear, but why should a spinner followed by a rubber fish succeed repeatedly? Before considering why a flounder

Movement rather than colour is the most important feature in allowing the flounder to detect its prey.

might select any particular bait or lure it is worth mentioning just one more observation. In the estuary of the River Frome in Dorset the youngsters fish from Wareham quay. They catch flounder after flounder on a wide range of tackles, particularly in early winter. Many of them bait their hooks with garden worms for, although the estuary is tidal, there is little or no salt water influence on most tides. Some, however, use the alternative bait of ragworm, generally purchased from the local tackle shop. The result of the bait change is a large increase in the number of bites and fish caught.

It is quite clear then that flounders, although they have catholic tastes, may be very fussy about what they eat. University of Bath researchers J. W. and I. A. Moore have studied the basis of food selection by these fish in the Severn estuary. It is already well known that the food of most fish (flounders included) varies from place to place because it depends on what is available. Within these limits the nature of the creatures eaten is governed by the time of year and the water conditions. The scientists sampled flounders from the intake screens of Oldbury nuclear power station. The water of the cooling lagoon, in which the fish were living, was generally pretty dirty (anyone who has fished the Severn will realise what an understatement that is) and the bottom was muddy sand. The prey animals living in the lagoon were mostly crustaceans, worms and molluscs ranging from the larger forms such as brown shrimps and red harbour ragworms to sand hoppers, Baltic tellins (little sand-burrowing clams), mysid shrimps, tiny but very active relatives of the woodlouse called *Eurydice* and small mud-snails such as *Hydrobia*.

In February the flounders fed chiefly on bottom-living harbour ragworms; from March to April they switched to beach fleas that closely resemble the well-known freshwater shrimp. Then, in the summer months, when they were feeding most actively, they chased, caught and ate the fast-swimming brown shrimps and the smaller but similar mysids. In summertime less of the fish had full stomachs because, although they ate more, they digested their food much faster.

To back up these observations the researchers carried out some experiments in tanks, using little water slaters as prey for the flatties. In one test the fish could detect prey both in dirty water and in clear water. The flounders searched by making short darts across the seabed, pausing between moves to look for potential prey (see the comments on plaice above). It is pretty obvious when the flatty spots its prey because its eyes flick about rapidly as it lines up its body for the strike. The strike itself is made with a smooth, swift, forward lunge.

Large flounders were able to see slaters almost twice as far away in clear water as in dirty water (14 in as opposed to 8 in). Whatever the colour of the water the flounders were still able to find very small prey, much smaller in fact than the baits used by anglers (which is perhaps just as well for anglers fishing the murky waters of places like the Severn estuary). It might take a fish up to four seconds to catch a large slater in dirty water, but the time needed was much less if the prey were close when they were detected. Freshwater shrimps, which are very active swimmers, escaped from as many as 20% of attacks, while the poor old, slow-moving slaters were caught every time. The very fast-swimming *Eurydice* escaped almost always.

Big brown shrimps are a decent mouthful and obviously desirable prey for the flounders, which easily see them and swim quickly towards them. The shrimps, however, are not impressed and dart away with a typical tail first escape reaction. In clear water this tactic is only successful in avoiding capture on about half of the occasions, but in dirty water the shrimps get away every time. When the water is cold (8°C), the flounders do not even bother to chase the faster-moving types of prey. Slower-moving life forms are just as vulnerable as in warmer conditions. Ragworms, it seems, are more likely to be eaten in cold winter seas. Movement rather than colour is the most important feature in allowing the flounder to detect its prey. This probably goes a long way to explaining the effectiveness of spinners and the like for catching these fish.

The baited spoon

Much of what is known about flounder fishing fits into the picture painted above. Most notable is the 'going down' described by Garrad in his experiments with baited spoons. This involves a shift from active summer feeding habits (which made flounders susceptible to his mobile trolling technique) to bottom feeding in winter, when legered and relatively inert baits were much more successful. It makes you think, doesn't it?

So have we attained the ultimate in shore fishing methods, particularly for flatties? Apart from casting a few yards further out and using slightly less conspicuous end gear than we did 20 years ago, how can we catch more fish? There are chemically sharpened hooks, bait additives and lots more books and magazines full of advice. Why, then, are fish not queuing up to be caught?

Like most anglers, we are always on the lookout for new and 'deadly' tactics. Despite the fact that our areas of experiment are generally restricted to the species available in our home area of south Dorset, results have often been spectacular. Buoyant plugs, poppers, soft plastics and free-lined baits used for bass have, at times, resulted in phenomenal success, and surface-fished maggot flies have also given us many red-letter days with mullet and bass.

One summer a few years ago we concentrated entirely on the use of baited spoons, spun from the estuary shore, for thin-lipped mullet. Although they had been developed in France many years earlier, these lure were, at that time, only used by anglers in the waters of Christchurch Harbour. After trying them in many other spots along the south coast we found that they were almost unbelievably effective. Interestingly, while we were mullet fishing, we picked up quite a few flounders, too.

Do these spinners work for flounders elsewhere? A few years back Mike had a chance to find out when he made his

The baited spoon can be effective for flounders when spinning from the shore.

A flounder caught on a ragworm baited mullet spoon. This lure has a lead body to assist casting, but plastic bead bodies are also fine.

annual relative-visiting pilgrimage to the northeast coast. At the time of his visit the fishing column in a local newspaper had said that flounders were 'the only hope for shore anglers' and the number of inactive rods lined up along the beach at Newbiggin confirmed that sport was not exactly hectic. What better testing ground than that for the baited spoons?

Mike visited Steve's Fishing Tackle in South Shields and bought a few ounces of ragworm; they were not sold by the dozen, as down south. A chat with the blokes behind the counter reinforced the impression that fishing was slow and he had nothing to lose, so the following morning he set off with wife, sons, worms and all to the seaside village of Alnmouth. Mike had not been to the estuary of the River Aln for 25 years, but he clearly remembered the sand dunes covered in marram grass and the river channel winding down across the golden beach to the sea's edge. It had not changed.

The sun spilled down and the family went their separate ways, leaving the old man to his daft experiments. He set up the spinning rod with 8 lb line and a size 5, silver-bladed and plastic-bead-bodied spoon, just as he would for mullet at home. No lead was needed, because the idea was to fish just fast enough to keep the blade turning. Trailing two inches behind the spoon was a small treble on the end of a short length of mono, and above that a size 12 single hook to retain the bait. The very first cast, upstream and across, was met by a double pluck – definitely a bite. As Mike reeled in, the plucking continued and the flashing spoon hove into view with a little brownish kite shape in its wake. The 6 in flounder turned away only when its new toy was lifted from the water. Encouragement – just what the doctor ordered.

Mike made his way along the river channel towards the sea, casting and retrieving every few paces. Several times little flounders followed and chewed at the ragworm, even ripping it off the hook once or twice, but all of them came adrift. By now it was low water and a couple of blokes brought their beach-casting gear down to do some (conventional) flounder fishing in the sea outside the river mouth. Little waves were rolling into the clear, shallow water over a sandy bottom. Mike waded out a few yards and carried on spinning. Ten minutes later, several more fish had tried but failed to hang themselves on the spoon.

There seemed to be nothing obviously wrong with the hook rig, but he changed the little treble for a chemically sharpened Aberdeen hook. Straight away it was obvious that this would assist baiting up. The hook point was inserted into the worm just behind its head and slid along until the small retaining hook above could be nicked in to the tough head region. On the very next cast, the familiar pluck, pluck, pluck turned into a hooked flounder.

In the following two hours, no fewer than eight fish were landed and only three were lost, unfortunately one of the escapees was the biggest of the bunch, about a pound. The flounders were all in the ounces category, and all went back in mint condition, a process not difficult to achieve as every one was lip-hooked.

So he only caught a few titchy flounders. We can almost hear the scathing remarks from you seasoned flattie-bashers, but don't be too hasty. It was probably not coincidence that the two blokes fishing standard leger tactics and resting their rods failed to get even a single bite. There is no reason why spinning should not work for flounders of all sizes, and unhooking big fish (always nicked in the mouth) will be even easier than dealing with the small ones. This is most important in a conservation-conscious age. Spinning is an active method that allows you to search large areas of water and attract fish from a distance. No doubt it could be a useful match tactic if anyone can withstand the inevitable ridicule as they try it out.

Hooking flatfish

A couple of emails in response to a question that Mike had posted on his website provide an insight into one of the best ways to fish for flatfish. Mike's question, posed in total ignorance, was: when full circle hooks were first introduced in the UK a number of writers said that they were more difficult to use with bait (or to bait up) than J hooks – does anyone know why?

The first answer came from the late Dave Bourne, for many years the shore-caught bass record holder, who at that time lived in Scotland. Now Dave was a top class all-round angler and anything he said was likely to be spot on. Dave had been using these hooks for about three years and his response to the question was as follows:

Threading on a worm is very difficult. I have been using full circle hooks and, being short shank and not offset at all, it's almost impossible to get a worm on whole. I'm thinking of trying the semi-circle hooks from Veals

> The use of circle hooks greatly reduces the numbers of flatfish killed by deep hooking.

this year to see if that is any better. I hope that answers the question I saw on your website – if not, try threading a ragworm on a size 2 full circle and you'll soon see the problem.

Of course, Mike should have tried it himself, but, to be honest, he had assumed that the worms could just be lip-hooked and allowed to dangle (see Mike Richards' email below). Of course, he was just being stupid. He had not considered that, with any form of distance cast, worms hooked in this way would simply fly off. Nevertheless, it is still possible to make short casts with head-hooked worms or to thread on sections of larger worms.

Following on from this – and most sea anglers will have fished for flatfish at some time – anyone who has legered for plaice, flounder or dab must have encountered the problem of deeply hooked fish. Flatties have smallish mouths and big appetites so they are apt to swallow the lot, which results in surgical operations to remove hooks and serious damage to the fish. This is no problem when the fish are to be eaten. However, often the specimens caught are undersized or immature and the resultant slaughter is totally unacceptable. Is there a solution?

Dave appears to have come to the same conclusion as us that circle hooks are good for fish conservation. He sent some other comments about his experiences with circle hooks, having used them, in smallish sizes, for plaice fishing for three years. He continued:

We get a good run of plaice in June up here and they are my favourite eating fish, but there are a lot of small fish caught and when using J hooks they are often deeply hooked. Circle hooks, as you know have solved most of this problem, but there is a real difficulty baiting up.

Undeterred by this difficulty, Dave went on to say that by offsetting the hook slightly (bending the point to one side) and using a baiting needle (modern type) it can be done, but it is very fiddly. He obviously thought that it was worthwhile, despite being fiddly, and he pre-baited his traces so that they were ready to just clip on when he reeled in, giving him more fishing time. He also commented:

The circle hook offset point seems OK. I have deep-hooked a couple of fish, but they were for the pot anyway. Even so it's nothing like as bad as it was with the J hook. I was thinking of stopping plaice fishing altogether with the by-catch that I was killing.

Another pal, Mike Richards, sent an email that made similar points:

The circle hooks are virtually impossible to thread lug and ragworms onto. They are usually very thick wired as well, which seems to pop the worms more. I've used circled (Varivas) hooks to good effect for bass and flatfish with ragworm and sandeel just nicked through the head, and flicked out 20–30 yards. The Varivas semi-circle hooks are a bit easier to thread worms onto, but they are still quite difficult. One hook pattern which I've been informed by a few people is the best to use to prevent deep-hooking of flatfish is called a 'Messler'.

The 'Messler' seems to be a fairly normal, short-shanked hook attached by means of a non-slip loop knot (the one we use for lures and big flies) so that it can swing freely on the nylon trace. We have to say that with the big live and dead baits we normally use for bass, perch, pike and so on, baiting up circle (or any other) hooks is never a problem. Note also the comments on using worm-baited circle hooks for wrasse.

A flounder taken on an artificial lure, showing that there's plenty of potential for catching these tasty predators.

We expect that we are biased, but here are two more very good anglers confirming that circle hooks (despite the baiting-up difficulties) can have massive benefits for certain types of fishing, notably for flatfish. Clearly they both think that it is worth taking a bit of trouble to try to solve the baiting problem.

It can only be a matter of time before Mr Average Angler cottons on to this and perhaps a year or two more before the manufacturers realise that there is a market for quality offset circle hooks and/or a different design to make baiting up easier – we would have a go at inventing one ourselves if we ever actually did much beach-casting with worm baits these days.

chapter_06

MACKEREL, SCAD, SHAD, MULLET AND GARFISH
THE LIGHT TACKLE ANGLER'S DREAM

MACKEREL

There are few things tastier than a fillet of mackerel. Grilled, poached, barbecued, fried or smoked, the old *Scomber scombrus*, fresh from the sea, is a meal fit only for gourmets and sea anglers. The secret of the mackerel's fantastic flavour lies in the fact that it is an oily fish with its own built-in aromatic basting. The sort of delicacy that a *cordon bleu* cook would be delighted to create – if only he knew how.

Because of its availability and strong fishy odour the mackerel is not simply a good meal, but is widely regarded (probably incorrectly so) as the universal bait. Most anglers seeking big fish usually choose a large oily mackerel fillet, although the fact that the mackerel bait smells strongly (to us) and often catches fish does not necessarily mean that it is always the best choice. In fact, for most sea fish, in the normal run of things, mackerel must be quite a rare meal.

Mackerel are mid-water to near-surface swimmers generally operating far above the hungry mouths of bottom-foraging cod, dogfish, rays, conger and the like. Yet despite these possible shortcomings, it is a fact that sea anglers devote a great deal of time, ingenuity and effort to the capture of these little fish.

It is possible to catch mackerel on tackle appropriate to their size, habits and hard-fighting capabilities. Angling authors often pay lip-service to such an approach, but the truth is that few people ever try to 'fish light'. Not so many years ago the trolled mackerel spinner was the traditional means of filling the bait box. Today the majority of fish are still caught on strings of hooks dressed with feathers, plastic tape or some other material intended to simulate small fish or other mackerel-food sized morsels.

In boat fishing, when the fish are thick on the ground, it may be possible to haul up full strings with little or no knowledge of the fish and minimal skill in handling tackle. Not so from the shore. You only have to spend a few hours on Chesil Beach during a hot summer day to see that some anglers have perfected the art of feathering from the shingle slope.

Stripped to the waist, the experienced mackerel man sits on the beach with his hat tilted over his eyes. All around him are anglers engaged in frenzied activity, casting and retrieving continuously, but landing only the occasional fish. When he judges that the time and tide are right our expert stands up, shakes the odd pebble out of his shorts and grabs his *fishing* tackle. The rod is no miracle of modern science, but a fairly stout 12 ft pole which has seen better days. On the butt is clipped a big fixed-spool reel, clearly intended to give him a brisk retrieve with minimum effort.

Body and rod flex in a powerful curve and the big lead wings its way out to sea, followed closely by a trail of glistening, opalescent, tape-clad hooks. With the rod held almost horizontally and pointing along the beach, the angler begins to crank the handle of his big reel and at the same time heaves the rod back and forth to give a 'sink and draw' motion to the lures. Within seconds, his rod takes on a steeper curve than that caused by the drag of lead and feathers.

As the rod swings into an upright position the retrieve is speeded up and, shortly, a chain of silver, iridescent, kicking fish is lifted from the surf to be unhooked with a few deft movements. With the minimum of time wasted the whole exercise is repeated and, twenty minutes later, our model angler is trudging up the shingle bank, rod in one hand and carrier bag well filled with supper and conger or bass bait in the other.

There is no doubt that, as a means of obtaining first-class bait and food, the method described above is very effective. However, all the anglers fishing the Chesil Bank could not compete with a single commercial fishing boat in terms of numbers caught. We are all well aware of the potential inroads modern fishing methods can make into stocks. The North Sea herrings were fished almost to extinction, and mackerel have recently threatened to go the same way.

Because of the obvious threat to mackerel in our seas, scientists in the UK and other European countries have recently turned their attention to the numbers, distribution, production and, in particular, the identity of separate stocks or groups which are present. For years it has been clear that the mackerel around the British Isles behave as though they are two distinct units. One of these groups of mackerel spawns in the middle of the North Sea. After breeding they migrate northwards to the summer feeding grounds and then rest, over winter, off the north of Scotland, before repeating the whole exercise. The so-called Western mackerel stock, which is responsible for most of our south coast sport, spawns off southwest Ireland, overwinters off northwest Ireland and feeds all round our coastline.

Due to the different sea areas in which they are born the offspring of the two stocks spend their early months in water of different temperatures and consequently they grow at quite different rates in their first year. This difference in growth leaves its mark on the fish. The ear bones (otoliths) are zoned with rings like those found in tree trunks and the first ring of a North Sea fish is much narrower, indicating slower growth, than that of its southern relatives.

It is also known that there are big differences between the changes in abundance of the two groups because of variation in year class strength and fishing effort. All of this suggests that the North Sea and Western mackerel stocks should be controlled separately in terms of quotas and other management restrictions.

However, recent scientific work, based on the modern techniques of genetic fingerprinting, have shown that, despite their differences in growth and behaviour, the two stocks belong to the same race and their genes are identical. In short, despite the importance of mackerel to the ecology and the economy of our seas, we are still woefully ignorant about many important details of their lives.

So what has any of this to do with our fishing? What we are trying to say is that next time you are shaking a full string of silver beauties into the fish box spare a thought for their well-being and stop when you have caught sufficient for your needs.

If you really want to make the most of mackerel fishing, from the point of view of sport, then your best approach may be light fly gear armed with a small streamer fly, Clouser minnow or plastic eel. You will catch even more if you spin with small wedges, spoons or plugs, but beware – these are delicate fish. Using single hooks with the barbs well flattened, mackerel can often be shaken back into the sea without touching their sensitive skins, but if they are badly hooked on a barbed treble hook you may as well kill them. We have often stopped fishing for them when they were biting well to avoid carnage.

Like so many other predators, mackerel bite best at dawn or dusk and these are the prime times to fish for them from the shore. When they are in the mood (which is often in warm, calm conditions) they will take almost anything, including large popping surface lures intended for bass.

> Mackerel bite best at dawn or dusk and these are the prime times to fish for them from the shore with fly gear and a floating line.

Fish colour

Mackerel are beautiful silver fish with rainbow colours dancing over their shining scales, but exactly what colour is a fish? It is a simple, possibly even silly, question but not so easy to answer as you might think. Just take shads as an example. Look in any textbook on British fishes and you will see pictures of these now rare and exciting fishes.

The brilliant iridescent colours of mackerel change as the fish turns and provide signals to co-ordinate the movements of other shoal members.

Shad are relatives of herrings and sprats and they could be (and often are) easily mistaken for decent-sized herrings. The features used to identify shads relate to things such as the number of gill rakers and similar obscure details. However, the book will show you that shads, unlike herrings, have dark spots, a bit like fingerprints, on their flanks. The allis shad, which, sadly, seems to be almost extinct in our rivers, has one spot and the twaite shad has a whole row of spots. What the book will fail to tell you is that the spots virtually disappear as soon as you lift the fish from the water and, like magic, reappear when you pop it back in. This trick was shown to us by the angling author Dave Lewis many years ago. It is exactly like those holographic images on your credit card that only appear when you view them at the correct angle.

So there is the first colour problem: fish in the water may look different to fish in the hand. An additional difficulty well-known to sea anglers is the way that the colours and patterns of fish rapidly change and fade as they die. A black bream or a pouting fresh from the sea will usually have dark vertical stripes on its body, but within minutes of being lifted into the boat the markings have gone. These changes are quite different to the pressure patterns that appear on the bodies of cod, conger and other fish as they lie in the fish box or on the bottom boards of a boat.

Scad have a white disc inside the mouth that shows other scad when they are feeding.

Even more transient are the fantastic violet sheens that overlay the bright silver scales of living salmon, sprats, herring and many other near-surface swimmers. These interference

Scad also have iridescent interference colours for signalling to feeding shoalmates. This one was used for livebait.

colours may last for only a few seconds after the fish is caught, so only a sharp-eyed angler is ever likely to see them. Other species may have green or gold iridescent overlays on the basic silver and still others, like mackerel and scad,

Mackerel and scad signal to shoalmates with iridescent colours on the flanks.

seem to be all colours of the rainbow. The skin of a living mackerel, for instance, looks as if it was covered with a thin film of oil, constantly changing colour as the fish moves its body from side to side.

Some colour patterns have very obvious functions such as camouflage or display. For example, most bottom-dwelling fish are, broadly speaking, coloured like the sandy or rocky seabeds over which they roam and many have a mottled pattern or disruptive markings that break up the fishy outline. In addition, the majority of fish are able to change colour so that even silvery surface dwellers like herring, bass and mackerel may adopt different shades of green, blue, grey or brown in dirty water or poor light. The past masters of colour change are flatfish, which are often able to match almost any seabed in a matter of seconds.

The contrasting spots and brightly coloured markings of some wrasses, breams, dragonets, gurnards and the like are clearly for displaying to the opposite sex or for bullying rivals. The bigger and brighter the pattern the better it tends to work. However, there is a serious drawback to this flamboyant display. Any fish that is unusually conspicuous is more likely to attract the attention of a predator. It is all a matter of swings and roundabouts.

Scad are attracted to lights at night and take flies and small spinners well where lamps shine onto the sea (docks, bridges, etc.).

Relatively recent discoveries are the hidden display colours of fish such as mackerel, sandeels and, particularly, scad. In the hand, freshly caught scad are essentially shiny green and silver in colour. The bright silver flanks, however, conceal red and yellow interference colours (again like the iridescence of a layer of oil on water). These hues are displayed to other members of the shoal as the fish turns, red-yellow, red-yellow, allowing shoalmates to synchronise their swimming.

Scad also have another trick of communication. Inside the mouth is a bright, shining white disc pattern that is only apparent to other members of the school when the fish has its mouth wide open during feeding. This seems to be a sort of dinner gong or 'come and get it' signal. Presumably there is a considerable advantage to scad in feeding together as a group.

Interestingly, scad are attracted to lights and may feed right at the surface under the street lamps on bridges, promenades and piers. This, together with their preference for plankton and other small food items, makes them prime candidates for nocturnal fly fishing. Experiments have shown that whiting also have an irresistible attraction to lights at night time, so it may not be long until we see anglers wielding fly rods from the beaches in the depths of winter.

Saltwater fly fishing

All of these relatively small species provide fantastic sport on fly tackle. Now we admit that we are no great fly casters. In fact, many of the fly fishermen we see can cast further, straighter and with much greater delicacy than we do ourselves. However, we do catch lots of fish on fly gear and we really enjoy playing and landing fish on fly tackle. The point we are trying to make is that, even if you have never tried it before, there is no need to be scared of attempting to fly fish in the sea. To start with it is probably worth having a few chucks in the local field, just to get the hang of extending a line, but there is certainly no need to spend a fortune on specialist rods, reels and lines just to give it a go. Mind you, don't let us stop you if you want to invest in pukka saltwater fly fishing gear.

Whatever you might be told, the basic reason for using fly tackle is not sportsmanship nor artistry – it is simply equipment designed to cast a small, virtually weightless, lure to where the fish are likely to be and that does not have to be more than 10 or 20 yards from the beach, rocks or pier. Any other sort of tackle would need added weight in the form of a sinker and/or float, just to get your almost weightless artificial to the fish, but in the case of fly gear all the weight is in the line. From the point of view of casting, the lighter the fly the better. In many ways, the heavy fly rods and reservoir style equipment used for casting heavily weighted lures (flies) is best left in the shop. In most situations where this sort of tackle would be effective you are probably better to use spinning gear and plugs or spoons. (For that matter, without wishing to raise anyone's hackles, quite often it would also be more effective to do this for reservoir trout.)

A small plastic eel used on fly tackle and the sand smelt, a bait fish it roughly resembles.

Small flies are not the only way to catch mackerel. This small 'joey' mackerel took a plug almost as large as itself.

Small plastic eels make excellent artificial flies for sea fish from mackerel and scad to bass and pollack.

In practice, we have done quite a bit of fly fishing. We use our fly tackle mainly for amusement, even though we know that we could often catch many more (and probably larger) fish on plugs, spoons or bait. Very few of the fish that we catch need even a moderate cast and most of them are only a few yards beyond the rod tip. We often do very little conventional casting – simply twitching out a few yards of line in a sort of pitiful roll cast, and retrieving by raising the rod and letting the weight of the fly line drag the lure through the water.

One of Mike's favourite 'flies' is a tiny Redgill or Delta eel and as an experiment on several occasions he tried two such lures, a natural (silvery-white) eel on the point and a black one (the same size) about one foot up the cast. The idea was not to catch two fish at once but to see whether the colour of the fly made any difference as the light changed. Trials like this add a bit of interest to the fishing and, with luck, could provide the answers to a few questions (see chapter 9 for more detailed information).

GARFISH

Garfish are often associated with mackerel. In the old literature they are frequently referred to as 'mackerel guides' or 'mackerel scouts'. Presumably they turn up earlier in the season than the mackerel themselves. Certainly garfish migrate into our coastal waters in spring and depart again in the autumn.

The brilliant silver scales of a garfish caught on a surface slider. Garfish provide good sport on fly gear.

The 'tweezer-like' beak of the garfish is armed with many sharp teeth for gripping small crustaceans and fish fry.

A Swedish study showed that garfish mostly ate slaters and beach hoppers, if they could get their beaks on them. They also fed heavily on juvenile herrings and sprats as well as sticklebacks (which occur in salt water and must be an easy catch for a fast-moving garfish) and sandeels. Garfish caught on rod and line from Courtmacsherry Bay in Ireland had been feeding on crustaceans, especially little transparent crab larvae, and they also ate young fish (mostly herrings and sprats).

Interestingly, garfish will take insects trapped in the surface film of the sea so, at times, anything from flying ants to seaweed flies must be potential food for them. The fish often regurgitated their stomach contents as they were being reeled in so the guts were frequently empty. Occasionally bits of paper, tinfoil and even cigarette ends were found in stomachs, suggesting that creating a suitable imitation to fool garfish would not be too taxing for the budding fly tier.

Most of the Swedish-caught garfish were young ones of up to four years of age, but a few were as old as ten or eleven years. The younger specimens might be about 25 in long, while the oldest probably attained 33 in. Female fish were usually a bit longer than males. In Ireland the size range of the garfish caught was similar, although one or two were almost 3 ft long and about 2 lb in weight.

MULLET

Spinning for mullet

Our pal Will was keen to catch a thin-lipped mullet. Perhaps because he was relatively new to fishing, Will's enthusiasm was second to none. When Mike phoned to suggest an early-morning start in search of thin-lips he swears he could hear Will winding up his alarm clock. The day dawned dull and damp and, as we (Mike, Will and Steve) walked down to the boat-launching ramp on the river, it began to rain. As we stowed the rods and tackle, we talked excitedly about the prospects.

An hour and a half and three different spots later, things were not looking so rosy. Apart from a jack pike that took Will's rag-baited spoon and neatly unhooked itself at the net, we were biteless. We had seen neither fin nor scale of the thin-lipped mullet we were aiming to catch.

Mike suggested a move downriver to a point where the salt water meets the fresh. Although we were well aware of the fact that the mixed water would probably be dirty, a move of this kind had, once or twice, saved the day, with fish caught at the spot we had in mind. Steve motored down to the wide bend in the river and dropped anchor in one metre of distinctly murky water near the end of a small drainage ditch.

The decision was soon justified by a howl of joy from Will, as a mullet followed his lure right up to the boat before turning away. It was not long before everyone was in action, with fish up to about 4 lb, and Will's face had to be seen to be believed when Steve netted his first-ever thin-lip for him.

The mullet were far from numerous on that day, but, as we fished, a strange thing occurred. We noticed one or two fish swimming at the surface with the tops of their heads, upper lips and eyes well proud of the water. Now we have seen thick-lips, on hundreds of occasions, taking seaweed fly maggots in just this way, but never thin-lips (since that time we have often seen thin-lips feeding on the surface in various parts of Poole Harbour). Before long, it was obvious that the surface feeders were restricted to a narrow 'wind lane' of brown scum in mid-river and within ten or fifteen minutes there were literally a hundred or more fish gobbling away in a few square yards of scummy shallow water. No doubt they could have been caught on a suitable scum-imitating dry fly.

> Thin-lipped mullet take ragworm-baited spoons well in rivers and estuaries; thick-lips can be tempted along the open shore.

Despite their surface-feeding activity the thin-lips were, nevertheless, interested in our rag-baited spoons. We caught and returned fish steadily until the appearance of Steve's wife Lynn, plus children, on the riverbank, told us that we had outstayed our time. It was a contented group of mullet spinners that motored back upstream to the slipway.

A few weeks after his mullet session Will had to visit Dorset again on business, and we invited him to spend a free day and a couple of nights with us in Wareham. Of course, fishing was again top of the agenda. There is no space to recount details of the whole 'fish in'. Suffice it to say that on this occasion we caught another bag of decent mullet from the dinghy. This time there was no obvious surface-feeding activity and fish were caught by letting the spinners sink for a few seconds before starting the retrieve, but the sport on the baited lures was just as exciting as it had been the time before.

Like thick-lips, the thin-lips battle it out and never give up. Thick-lips are much less easy to tempt with baited spinners than their freshwater-tolerant

A lead-bodied, ragworm-baited mullet spoon. The worm is nipped off at the bend of the rear hook. When you feel a plucking bite just keep winding steadily.

relatives. However, there are times when the method works well for them. This is particularly the case in flat calm, gin-clear conditions. We will give an example: Mike's son Richard wanted to try an afternoon mullet session with us on the Purbeck coast, in low water, flat calm, gin-clear, blazing-sun conditions. Everything was wrong for our usual mullet tactics (maggot fly). Still we went for the thick-lips again, but this time with ragworm-baited bar-spoons.

We made our way to where the wrack-clothed ledges were covered by only a couple of feet of water. Sure enough the mullet were out there basking and occasionally splashing at the surface. Paddling out to within easy casting range, about ten yards, we began to work the home-made, rag-baited spinners. Mike had a bite on the first cast and spirits rose. Minutes later he was playing a three-pounder as he backed carefully towards the shore. We unhooked and returned the fish and as we paddled back out the fish were still there. In the next half-hour all of us hooked, landed and lost decent specimens in a hectic session. When the tide began to rise, the mullet stopped biting and thinned out, presumably preparing for the high-water maggot fest.

All three British mullets are something of an enigma. Pick up almost any sea fishing book or magazine and you will find the same (mis-)information: 'difficult', 'wary', 'grey ghosts', 'freshwater tackle', 'soft mouths' and so on. Inevitably, all this perceived wisdom puts many people off even trying to catch mullet. Fair enough, as that leaves more for us to catch, but when was the last time you had a bite on a cast from hefty, hard-fighting fish? When was the last time you played a fish for five or ten minutes and were relieved to see it slide ashore? When were you surprised that the fish you thought was a 6 lb bass turned out to be a feisty scrapper of half that size? Bet you can't remember.

Put it another way: would you like to feel the excitement of a bending, bucking rod and hear the wild buzzing of the reel's clutch? If the answer is yes, then mullet are the fish for you.

Mullet on the fly

If you really want to know more about catching mullet we would advise you to join the National Mullet Club, but to give you a taste of the action we will describe another fishing trip, the one which turned out to be the catalyst for our film-making adventures. It started with a note lying on Mike's front doormat: 'Will be trying to video a mullet session Saturday night, high water is at seven o'clock, see you down at Flat Ledge. Steve.' Again Richard was keen to join us, so we packed a 12 ft float rod, fitted with a small fixed-spool reel, loaded with 4 lb line, a 'loafer' type float and some size 12 hooks. The other outfits were fly rods with #7 weight floating lines and 8 ft leaders of 6 lb nylon, each carrying a buoyant maggot fly dressed with a cylinder of polyethylene foam around a size 12-eyed hook. This unusual collection of fishing gear was assembled in the knowledge that surface-feeding mullet consistently gather in places where piles of rotting weed laced with seaweed-fly maggots line the high-water mark during the bimonthly spring tides.

Mike set to and threw a few armfuls of composted weed and maggots into the sea to try to get the fish going. An angler from Shaftesbury, armed with a fly

A thick-lipped grey mullet taken on a polyethylene maggot fly fished 'dry'. Live maggots on the bend of the hook make a big difference to the number of bites.

A fine thick-lipped mullet caught on the maggot fly. Captor: Jamie Baxter.

rod, was already scanning the surface of the sea for feeding fish. Steve shot a few minutes of tape to capture Mike's weed chucking style and to demonstrate the speed with which maggots could burrow back into the murk once they had been uncovered. For half an hour we waited and watched, but nothing came to the groundbait and we were just giving up hope when we spotted a shoal of mullet feeding 50 yards to our right.

A quick stumble along the shore and half a dozen casts with the fly gear and Mike was into a mullet. After filming for a while Steve picked up the landing net, but as he turned back towards the source of the action the line went slack. Stoically, Mike baited up with another bunch of maggots and began to cast again, hooking another hard-fighting thick-lip almost at once. This time Steve filmed the whole fight, with the guy from Shaftesbury taking care of the netting at the critical instant. The fish was landed, unhooked and returned to the sea.

Richard returned to tell us he had spotted some big fish feeding at the other end of the bay. It seemed that a fair number of mullet were mopping up maggots in the curling waves only a couple of feet from the water's edge. Out went the float tackle and Steve was shortly able to film the entire battle with a fish taken on the long rod and fixed-spool reel – equally as exciting as the fly fishing episode. If you want tense, nail-biting excitement in your sea angling, there is no doubt that, using the right tackle, mullet are the fish to give you the run-around with a guarantee of fast and furious action.

> Thin and thick-lipped mullet can both be caught on suitable fly tackle, spinning gear and freshwater set-ups.

chapter_07

POUTING, WHITING, POLLACK AND COALFISH
PESTS AND POWERHOUSES

POUTING

Tiddler snatching

'Pout and rockling continue to dominate', 'poor returns – a few rockling and pout showing', 'pout provided the action', 'good sport with pouting and poor cod'... Comments such as these often loom large in the angling columns of local south-coast newspapers. This is particularly the case in late winter and early spring, but even during other, more productive fishing seasons the humble pouting is a major element of catches along the shores of southern England. Whether, like us, you are simply catching one or two bass/cod/conger baits or, like many others, trying to scratch for a place in a match, the pout is frequently the number-one fish.

Now we have caught our fair share of pouting, both from the shore and from boats. Many a time we have been thrilled to feel the first rattling tugs of *Trisopterus luscus* on the end of the line. There can be few south coast sea anglers who have not sat and watched the immobile rod tip and prayed for the onset of dusk and the almost inevitable invasion of the pouting hordes. This little member of the cod family is one of the few species which is sufficiently abundant (and bites often enough) for us to form an impression of what is going on down below.

It soon becomes very obvious to anyone who casts a worm from the beach or dangles a small bait below a boat that the pouting is active mainly at night. It is also evident that the bites tend to come in bursts. Periods of frantic fish catching are interspersed with lulls in the action. This raises the question what the pouting are doing when they are not savaging our baits.

Of course, this is the $64,000 question in all fishing. Have the fish gone? If so, where have they gone? Have they just stopped feeding? If you read the angling magazines you will find plenty of experts with strong opinions. They will often state in no uncertain terms that the fish lie in the lee of sand banks waiting for their prey to be swept by, move off as the tide turns or stop feeding when the wind is in the east, etc. At best, such impressions are based on a wealth of angling experience and at worst (and more often), they are simply hearsay and hardly worth the paper they are written on. Hardly ever has anyone tried to relate pulls on the line to known and proven fish behaviour.

You might be thinking why should we care whether the fish have (a) shifted or (b) stopped eating? Clearly, it makes a big difference to what you should do if you want to catch rather than go home empty-handed. If your chosen species is still down there but has actually stopped eating you could change tactics and try for something else. If on the other hand, your target fish has simply moved a few hundred feet to the right, you should be walking, rowing, motoring or casting to the new spot.

Let's return to the pouting as our example. Scientists have actually observed and logged the changing activities of these fish with shifts in time and tide. Artificial reefs, plonked down in the middle of sandy, seabed 'deserts' act as pouting refuges (wrecks, oil rigs and natural reefs operate in exactly the same way). Thousands of the little fish may congregate over, in and around such a small sheltered oasis. The research findings are riveting and very useful to us as anglers. It seems that:

- In the hours of daylight the pout will hang around rocks.
- The harder the tide is running, the closer to the reef or structure they will be.
- Towards high or low water, as the flow eases off, the fish will move a bit further afield.

In addition:
- The pout seek shelter from the flow behind the rock piles. Particularly when there is a strong flow of water the fish will be in the lee of the hummock.
- At dusk, as light fails, the fish suddenly disperse to forage over the surrounding area.

In daytime, when the tide is running hard, pouting stay very close to reefs, rocks and wrecks.

In a fast tide the pouting will shelter in the lee of the reef.

These few simple facts provide us with a great deal of valuable information. If you want to catch pouting (they do make good bass baits) the significance of the observations is clear. If, like us, you wish to hook a big predator such as a bass you and your baits or lures could do worse than to follow the pouting, because the bass/cod/pollack/conger/coalfish almost certainly will.

*Pouting are important food fish for many predators. This one took a big fly.
Captor: Silas Maitland. Picture: Steve Binckes.*

Of course, the pouting is only one prey species and if you are to succeed as a sea angler with any regularity, you will need to find out about many others. We regard pouting as bait for

> As night falls the pouting spread out from their reefs to feed.

bass, pollack and conger and thanks to the work of marine scientists we now know just a bit more about the activities of these little fish.

WHITING

These small but fiercely predatory fish have also been studied by scientists, to see whether they eat different foods at different times of the day. Whiting feed mostly on other fish or on shrimps and crabs with a few worms and brittle stars thrown in as appetisers. In the North Sea the main fish eaten by whiting (in order of decreasing importance) were: smaller whiting, herring, dabs and sprats. The chief crustaceans eaten were swimming crabs, krill (a sort of swimming shrimp that is the main food of many whales) and shrimps.

Animals such as dabs, shrimps and crabs, by their nature, live mostly on the seabed and bury themselves in the sand during the day. The whiting ate these mostly when they were out and about at night. In contrast, krill (presumably also sprats and herrings), which rise towards the surface of the sea at night, were eaten mostly at dawn or in the evening, when they tend to swim down near the bottom. Young whiting were devoured by their fathers, mothers, aunts and uncles mostly in daylight.

Other scientific studies have confirmed that whiting are active more or less throughout the entire 24 hours, that 85% of the food consumed by good-sized whiting consists of fish and that less fish are generally eaten at night. All this suggests that moving fish baits should be most effective during the daytime and crab or shrimp at night. It is no surprise then that if you read the angling press, you will find that the experts generally advise budding whiting anglers to 'tip your worm baits with a strip of fish' in a desperate attempt to cater for all eventualities.

> Whiting feed throughout the day and night, mostly on other fish, particularly smaller whiting.

POLLACK

The sea is flat calm under a sun that blazes down from a clear blue sky. Along the rocky shore one or two anglers are float-fishing for wrasse, almost the only hope of a catch under these circumstances. A small boy stands at the water's edge and attempts to skim flat stones as his mongrel dog races in and out of the water yapping wildly. His parents are spread-eagled on big towels on the upper shore, their bodies glistening in the bright light and enveloped in a haze of coconut-scented suntan oil.

No doubt most of us have, at one time or another, encountered similar scenarios. As we stood or sat by our rods, staring at the point where the filament of nylon line curved in to the surface film of the clear water, we may have noticed that the smooth surface had been disturbed by a patch of tiny wrinkles moving in a steady, purposeful manner against the tidal flow. Perhaps the cause of the wrinkles was revealed when a shower of little silver fry exploded from the water under the onslaught of a mini-pollack launched from the bladder-wrack bed as it gently swayed six inches under the surface.

There is no sport to be had from tiny surface-swimming fry, but there are lessons to be learned if we are able to recognise them. The first thing to realise is that there are two different kinds of little fish. Firstly there are the true midgets of the undersea world: sprats, sandeels, gobies, sand-smelts, sticklebacks and the like. These small species are vulnerable throughout their lives to the attacks of larger fish, squids, crustaceans, jellyfish and anemones. Sea birds devour them in huge numbers, too. To make up for the numbers that, inevitably, are killed and eaten each year most of these 'forage fish' produce lots of young and, because they are short-lived and quick-growing, are capable of replacing massive losses by the following year.

The second group of small fry consists of the young stages of all the larger species with which we are so familiar. These are the ones that we aspire to catch when they are bigger. Everything from the humble five-bearded rockling to the mighty halibut starts out its days as a tiny transparent hatchling or larva. Only a few species, such as the herring, produce eggs that sink to the

A small pollack caught on a wedge. Pollack usually plunge after being hooked so their kelpy haunts can be a graveyard for lures.

seabed and lie there in sticky clumps; the rest release eggs that drift near the water surface or in mid-water, carried here and there with the currents until they hatch.

The majority of these free-floating eggs are minute. They are so small that a decent-sized female fish may produce many millions of them every year after it reaches maturity. The resulting billions of tiny larvae are all competing for the available food resources. Those that are hatched early in the season have the advantage of a flying start and, if conditions are favourable, may be big enough to prey on the later arrivals or to bully them in the battle for food. The downside is that cold water will slow their growth, early-season rough seas may damage or disperse them and if the plankton on which they must feed is late to bloom or even fails completely they may starve to death.

Each species has evolved its own strategy designed to counter the problems of survival. For example, plaice spawn in winter, flounder in the spring, brill and turbot in the summer. The lesser sandeel is an autumn spawner, while its greater cousin waits until the spring and so on. In fact, there is, more or less, a complete sequence of new life appearing throughout the year. It follows from this that one or another type of small fish is present in our seas during every month, but, because the summer growing season is favourable for the majority of forms, it is in the warmer period that small fry are most abundant.

A wonderful fly-caught pollack. Captor: Silas Maitland. Picture: Steve Binckes.

It seems likely that the young of most species play a desperate game of cat and mouse (mostly mouse), not only with the weather and their food supply but also with their main predators. If they win, large numbers survive and the year class is a successful one; if they lose, our future prospects of a big catch in years to come are bleak.

Timing is not the only art needed for survival in the world of the juvenile fish. Subtle differences in behaviour enable each species to gain access to its favoured habitat. The larvae of bass, for example, drift into estuaries and accumulate where fresh and salt waters meet – a region that few other fry are able to tolerate. Cod larvae in the North Sea move from the spawning grounds, drifting inshore along an almost circular route until, by the time they are ready to begin foraging near the seabed, they have returned to the shallow coastal water. Conger larvae drift back to Britain from the deep water off the Azores where their parents migrated to spawn and then died. Such examples of each species finding its perfect niche are almost limitless.

One of the best documented examples of a successful survival strategy relates to the pollack. Mike wrote about this some years ago, but it bears repeating. We have only to look at the angling press to see that large mature pollack collect offshore for spawning in the early part of the year. Catches of monster pollack increase sharply in the period from January to March,

A more typical pollack taken from the shore on a fly fished Delta eel. Early-morning sessions often produce a fish a cast.

if the weather permits charter boats to visit wrecks off the southwestern approaches.

When the offspring of those mighty rod-benders first appear inshore, they are only capable of eating tiny crustaceans and other organisms they pick delicately from the weeds growing in shallow water. Even when they are very small, pollack have broad tastes and by the time they reach 6 in or so in length, they are inclined to impale themselves on our baited hooks when in search of a meal. The eager biting habits of these tiny fish disguise their true food preference, which is for the even smaller, near-surface-swimming two-spot gobies. Gobies ripple the calm waters around beds of kelp or eel grass and the tactics of the hunting pollack involve chasing the shoals of little prey fish through clearings in the weed. This hunting method is very successful because the pollack are strong swimmers. However, the pollack grow quickly and, before long, gobies are inadequate food.

Because they now need stronger meat the baby pollack have to switch their diet and the next convenient prey consists of tiny lesser sandeels. Unfortunately for the pollack, the sandeels are much stronger swimmers than the gobies and simply chasing them around is almost futile, so the crafty little hunters have to adopt a different approach. They change from being chasing hunters to ambush predators.

The pollack now lie in wait in the cover of convenient rocks or weed, to pounce out and take the passing sandeels by surprise. Good hiding places are so important that the little fish compete fiercely for the best lies (shades of the chalk stream trout). The pollack continue to grow quickly on the rich diet of sandeels and by the autumn they have become too big to survive solely on a diet of such small fry. Their feeding habits change once again, from solitary assassins to pack hunters.

At about 10 in long they school up and set about eating a wide variety of mid-water fish species such as sprats. The bigger pollack now move off into deeper water, but they may return later to raid the inshore reefs or to forage along gale-whipped winter beaches. Most of this fascinating story was unravelled by Potts and Wooton of the Marine Biological Association, and it would be a real treat to have similar information for our other sport fish. For certain, every species – cod, plaice, bass, whiting and the rest – has its own chain of development in which the links determine its success or failure and thus, in turn, dictate the future fortunes of our pastime with rod and line.

Pollack sometimes have very strong year classes and scientists Claridge and Potter noted that the young fish of 1974, a good year for breeding, were smaller than those in 1975 and 1976, which were poor survival years. Presumably the fish grew more slowly when there was greater competition for food. Local crashes in the abundance of these fish have also been reported from time to time.

Spent (spawned out) adult pollack migrate inshore in April and can be common on reefs by the beginning of May. From June onwards, inshore pollack become wanderers and will venture a long way from their rocky homes, particularly when they are hunting for the wandering shoals of sprats or herrings. In autumn, when heavy seas pound the coast and the water is filthy with suspended sediment, big pollack sometimes move close inshore and this gives the best chance of catching a double-figure fish from the beach or rocks.

Pollack are colourful fish. When they are young the basic olive-brown background is often enhanced by freckles of reddish-gold and blue, iridescent lines and spots. Surprisingly, older pollack also vary quite a lot in colouration. The colour appears to change not only with the surroundings but also with the depth of water (greyish to greenish olive in deeper water) and with the sea temperature (greener when its cooler). The tiny black spots which sometimes adorn the skin of small pollack are caused by a parasitic fluke, *Cryptocotyle lingua*.

If you want to catch pollack it is essential to fish in the right places. In April, one-year-old pollack often move close inshore along the south coast. At dusk, in calm weather, they dimple the water surface and will take small lures or, better still, artificial flies fished on fly tackle.

In summer the larger but still immature pollack tend to favour rocky, weedy ground in shallow water. In winter, as spawning time approaches, they will be found over sandy and muddy bottoms in depths of 90 m or more. Pollack feed mostly on other fish, but they are also partial to ragworms (particularly in springtime when ragworm spawn) and crustaceans of various kinds. As well as the usual free-swimming foods, pollack often take bottom-living animals such as rocklings, wrasses, shrimps and prawns. In the estuaries of large rivers pollack will feed heavily on salmon and sea trout smolts as they migrate downstream to the sea, chiefly in April and May.

> Pollack feed mainly in the early morning. They take flies and lures well at both dawn and dusk.

Although they are largely solitary, hunting adult pollack will band together and drive small prey fish into a tight ball near the surface of the sea. Gut analyses show that these fish feed mainly in the early morning. Generally by the afternoon their stomachs are almost empty or contain only the remains of the last meal. In the daylight pollack swim near the seabed and hide among the weeds and rocks, but at dawn and dusk they again rise towards the surface and will take shallow-fished baits or lures well into darkness. These are certainly the times when the fly fisher should ply his trade.

Pollack probably mature when they are only three or four years old. Fish of more than about 14 in in length are quite likely to be capable of spawning. The fish grow quickly and by the time they are ten years old may be well over 3 ft in length. They are not particularly flavoursome to eat (whatever Rick Stein or Hugh Fearnley-Whittingstall might say) and it is often thought that they taste much better, presumably of smoke, after they have been smoked.

Pollack reach more than 20 lb in weight, but for most shore anglers a 4 lb specimen is a very good fish. Their growing season is mostly between April and September. In the winter period the growth slows down a great deal. The scales of the pollack are small and, like many other members of the cod family, the growth rings are quite difficult to read. However, because the fish grow quickly the younger fish can often be aged approximately from their body lengths as follows:

- 1 year = 6–8 in
- 2 years = 10–11 in
- 3 years = 13–14 in and so on.

Pollack have large eyes and excellent dim-light vision. The senses of smell and taste are of less importance in feeding and captive pollack are alleged to have gulped down food soaked in turpentine, alcohol and chloroform. Despite this apparent disregard for the smell of their prey, blind fish have been observed to find their food by scent alone.

Like some other members of the cod family, pollack have a special set of muscles attached to the swim bladder, which enable them to make snoring or crooning sounds. The 'voice' of the pollack is used to communicate with other members of the species. Their snores are quite different from the sounds made by cod, coalfish and other noisy species.

Pollack rely largely on the lateral line sense (which detects vibrations) and on their acute vision to catch prey. Fish feeding in tank conditions seemed to

A young pollack caught on fly tackle. Note the blue spots, which are lost as the fish gets older.

be oblivious to the scent of their food. Pollack take rubber eels, jelly eels, shads, pirks and spoons keenly, but it is less well known that they are often caught in shallow water on plug baits, particularly at dusk. Their habit of plunging down into the kelp stems with £12 (or nowadays up to £25) worth of plug in their jaws might make them unpopular with pluggers. Despite their watery flesh, pollack, especially live ones, make good baits for predatory species such as bass and conger.

As you might expect from the above, the pollack has always been noted as very susceptible to lures. In the early part of the twentieth century angling writer Percy Wadham said that the pollack was one of the 'best takers of an artificial bait'. In years gone by, one of the outstanding baits for pollack was said to be a piece of sole skin or gurnard skin cut into a fish shape, but, according to Minchin (another angling writer), a double piece of parchment was an even better lure.

The well-known fad for black plastic eels as pollack lures is not new and in the late nineteenth century black rubber eels 'of the smallest size' were popular pollack baits. In 1911 an advertisement by Hearder & Son of Plymouth reports a catch of 388 pollack in three days. The fish weighed between 6.5 lb and 11 lb each and were taken on 'Hearder's spinning (rubber) sandeels'.

Our own experience with pollack suggests that one of the best baits of all is a little snotty freshwater eel (sadly in decline and now illegal to use) free-lined or spun on leadless tackle. At one time the newborn young of the spur dog (which have also become quite a rarity) were also regarded as prime pollack baits.

Pollack are very aggressive feeders, striking at prey from below. Several writers have described how large pollack rush upwards, often clearing the water, in pursuit of the silvery bubbles in a boat's wake.

COALFISH

Coalfish really are very similar to pollack in many ways. Once upon a time, flounders and coalfish were Mike's favourite species. As a lad he spent hours trying to catch them and relates that the thousands of fish he hooked and landed were fantastic sport. The coalies were not the wreck-haunting monsters that occasionally decorate the colour and news pages of the angling press, but the more ordinary creatures, which swim in the inshore waters off the northeast coast of England.

If you try to fish with ragworm or herring, crab or mussel, anywhere in the region of weed, rocks or harbour walls around our northern shores it will not be long before you feel the tug of a green-backed beauty on the end of your line. Your strike will be followed by a racy fight and, if the tackle is appropriate to the size of the fish, several minutes of entertainment may result.

Like pollack, inshore coalfish generally come in well-ordered sizes so that it is easily possible to predict how big the fish will be. After spawning in late winter to spring, mostly in deep water, the eggs float near the surface of the sea and hatch in about a week. The fry soon move inshore for protection and grow very quickly, reaching about 6 in in length by late summer. These little bait stealers can be a real nuisance to anglers after bigger and better fish, because they feed on worms, shrimps, small fish and anglers' baits as if there were no tomorrow.

One- to three-year-olds are the ones that usually get caught by shore anglers and, depending on the time of year and age, range from 8 in to almost 18 in long. The bigger fish can be quite a handful on lightish tackle. In their third winter, they mostly move offshore and are unlikely to be caught by shore anglers again.

Large coalfish feed mainly on other fish.

Large coalfish feed almost entirely on other fish, although when free-swimming shrimps are abundant they will gorge on them. Sprats, herrings and sandeels are the staple diet in most cases, so the best bet for luring a decent specimen is a fish bait, natural or artificial. Fish strips, livebaits, rubber eels, plugs, spoons, spinners and flies will all tempt coalies and, at times, a string of mackerel feathers produces fish after fish.

Mike recalls one occasion, fishing from the massive stone piers of Craster's little harbour in Northumberland. A ragworm bait or piece of herring flesh cast onto the sandy patches produced thumping great flounders and, over the rocks, down by the base of the stonework, the same bait would be taken by plump coalfish, which were at least two years old. A switch to feathers doubled the catch rate of coalies and added several bigger three-year-olds that had obviously lost their way.

It is now many years since Mike smelt the kipper fumes of Craster and, indeed, since he caught coalfish of any size. His current patch on the south coast of England is near the southern limit of coalfish distribution. Unlike their more northerly brethren, English Channel coalfish move offshore as one-year-olds and are almost entirely replaced by the much more numerous pollack.

One example shows what is possible, even in the south of England. It was mid-April and Harry had twisted Mike's arm into trying an early-season bass fishing session. They tackled up with buoyant plug baits on carp rods, fixed-spool reels and 8 lb lines and set out along a stretch of rocky shoreline. The beach was a mixture of cobbly stretches, ledges, lengths of boulder-strewn rock, thickets of tough weed and little shingle backed coves. Harry stopped on a short stretch of shingle and began to cast and retrieve a 6 in dark green Rebel plug with a red fluorescent belly stripe. Mike continued on his way to fish a long flat ledge using a black-and-silver J11 Rapala. Conditions were perfect with clear water, a strong flow of tide and a steady, though lively surf, but an hour of hard fishing produced no bites.

Mike made his way back to the spot where he had left Harry casting. As he rounded a jutting buttress of cliff he caught sight of his friend just as he swung a wriggling fish to hand. He quickened his pace and arrived as Harry was about to free his catch; he held it out for inspection and it was unquestionably a coalfish.

During the following 30 minutes, as dusk fell over the calm sea, they managed to catch half a dozen coalies, all in mint condition and looking like peas in a pod. The whole exercise was more interesting than exciting because the little fish were ridiculously overmatched by the carp rods and lines. As night drew in the shoals of coalfish began to show on the flat surface of the water, ringing and ruffling the sea like a group of rising trout.

They killed a few of the bigger fish to freeze down for conger and bass baits and, after they had packed in, Mike gutted a couple of fish to examine their stomach contents, in the hope of finding what had attracted them inshore. The guts were crammed with maggots; obviously the coalies were filling the gap occupied by surface-feeding grey mullet later in the year.

The good weather continued and, two days later, Mike and Harry were down at coalfish corner again, knowing that there was a good chance of a repeat performance, because fish are creatures of habit. Harry, as always, was again fishing a large plug in the hope of catching a big predator and Mike was armed with a trout fly rod, floating line and 8 ft of 5 lb nylon attached to the fly.

Mike's first cast was with a tiny black Delta eel in place of a more conventional fly. The tide was only halfway in so he was really just warming up his casting muscles. Cast and retrieve, cast and retrieve. Harry, meanwhile, was ten yards to his left pitching his plug well out to sea, probably about three times the fly gear's maximum range.

Coalfish like this are common in our northern inshore waters and can be fine sport for shore anglers. Picture: Dave Fitzpatrick.

After about five minutes of near-surface fishing, Mike decided to try a little deeper. To judge the sinking rate of his fly he flicked it out at his feet and counted as it sank through the water – eight seconds to reach the seabed. He worked out some line, made a modest cast and waited for the fly to sink. After a count of eight he raised the rod steadily to set the Delta in motion. The line was already tight and a fish was on! The battle was a short one, with the fish sheering right and left in the manner of a big dace. Mike swung it to hand and removed the fly, which was firmly lodged in the angle of the jaw. His catch was a 10 in coalfish in prime condition, but it was a flash in the pan because neither of them had another bite until the light began to fail.

By this time Mike had changed to a silver-bodied fry fly and Harry was legering with ragworm bait. In the following hour the fish went berserk and Mike landed 11 more, plus a couple of pollack for make-weights. In the course of catching the fish, at least three times as many were missed or made good their escapes – an excellent evening's sport. Harry's contribution was a single coalie on the worm; his only bite of the session apart from a couple of indeterminate pulls on the plug.

The moral of the above session is not that Mike is a better angler than Harry (he is not) nor that fry flies are more effective than Delta eels, ragworms or plugs, but simply that the right method, in the right place, at the right time will give the best results. If small coalfish can give decent sport on trout gear, then the bigger ones, which are so prolific in our northern waters, are a potential

Pollack and coalfish move offshore when they are older.

source of outstanding entertainment to anyone with the nerve to wield a fly rod or light spinning tackle from the rocks in the evening or, preferably, early-morning light. Of course, a 6–8 oz cod stick is a more conventional choice of weapon in these places.

Fish do not always have an easy life. A good example of the problems that may influence their search for food is revealed by the work of fishery scientists Carruthers, Neilsen, Waters and Purley who studied the diet and feeding habits of coalfish from the Bay of Fundy in the northwest Atlantic over several decades – now that is a long study. During this period there was a decrease in the abundance of the euphausiids (a type of big free-swimming shrimp) that the coalies sometimes ate. The stomach contents of 2,078 coalfish collected during 1958–1967 and of 1,230 more collected during 1996–2002 showed that, in the recent years, coalfish ate fewer shrimps than in the past and, overall, feeding activity had decreased. During the early period, shrimps were present in 65% of the coalfish stomachs that contained food but in only 9% in the later time period. There was no compensating increase in the amount of fish eaten. Empty stomachs were more common in the recent times during both winter and summer. It was concluded that the near-absence of shrimps in recently collected coalfish stomachs reflected low prey abundance. At the same time as the changes in diet and feeding intensity took place the condition or plumpness of coalfish also declined; in other words, they got skinnier.

Canadian scientists have studied coalfish using a split-beam echo sounder and bottom-trawl samples. They found that the fish spawn from January to March. They gather close to the seabed for spawning and stay in the same area, crowding tightly together at night and spreading further afield in daytime. Coalfish of similar size tend to stick together in shoals. The biggest fish are usually further offshore. After hatching the young coalfish move inshore for two to four years before heading out to deeper water.

Tagging showed that the young coalies tend to hang about on the same reefs while they are inshore, only moving a bit further afield to feed each day. Coalfish have a tendency to feed well above the seabed. Like other members of the cod family, they generally move further from the shore in winter.

When 6,000 young coalfish were tagged off Iceland it was again confirmed that they move about very little and in this case 53% of the fish were recaptured more or less where they had been tagged.

In Loch Ewe, Scotland, the habits of coalfish and pollack were compared using acoustic tracking, TV cameras and by examining stomach contents. The average swimming speed of young coalies is about 3ft/s (faster at night) but can increase up to 10ft/s when they are feeding. In open water, coalfish swim faster than pollack and range further from the reef during the daylight hours. Around kelp forests, coalfish feed in actively swimming shoals and take prey from the kelp while pollack are solitary and use the kelp only for cover.

A 14 lb 8 oz pollack taken on a fly. Captor: Steve Binckes. Picture: Silas Maitland.

Coalfish also take a wider range of prey than pollack and while they eat lots of amphipods (like beach hoppers), the pollack prefer mysid shrimps. So by adopting different hunting strategies, using habitat differently and having selective prey preferences, coalfish and pollack are able to live together in the same areas.

chapter_**08**

SHARKS, RAYS AND DOGFISH
SWIMMING
CIRCUIT BOARDS

SHARKS

Where's my shark gone?

It was going to be a superb day, one of those when the sea sparkles in the summer sunshine and all is right with the world. As we left Weymouth harbour, Mike's watch was showing 05:55 and the mist was just lifting from the seafront under the influence of the sun's slanting rays from the east. Out on the Shambles Bank, a small neap tide was swirling and lifting into little overfalls and whirlpools over the great dunes of shell and grit that formed the seabed. The other two blokes on the charter were keen to catch turbot or brill and had tackled up accordingly, with long traces and slender belly strips of fresh mackerel, designed to imitate the shape and movement of sandeels.

Mike was being obstinate (as usual) and had determined to try to tempt a tope. His gear was not all that different, a 12 ft trace of 15 lb nylon and a link swivel leger so that the weight could be changed quickly to suit the flow. But he added a couple of feet of nylon-covered wire and a well-sharpened 4/0 hook, while his bait was a whole freshly caught mackerel hooked through the wrist of the tail.

We fished on the drift, motoring uptide, cutting the engine and allowing the current to trundle our baits across the undersea landscape where (hopefully) the daytime predators lay in wait for, or were already harrying, the shoals of little forage fish. The day was as good as the early signs had promised in all but results. True, we caught plenty of fish – mackerel, scad, garfish, a couple of bass and even a small turbot, but for three or four hours Mike tended his tackle without even the semblance of a bite. By this you will gather that he is well known to be stubborn (even pig-headed) when it comes to fishing, but he was determined to stick to his big livebait – there must be a tope down there somewhere.

It was not until late in the afternoon that his patience was rewarded, but even then it was not quite what he expected. At the end of a long drift everyone retrieved their tackle in preparation for the next move uptide. The engine was started but was left out of gear until everything was in the boat. The other anglers were way ahead of Mike and began to scoff at his slowness. Now he was suffering for the amount of line that he had let out. The spool of the multiplier seemed to fill at snail's pace and everyone peered at the sea for the first glimpse of the mackerel bait. There it was, a silvery white flash, deep in the clear water.

Suddenly a long, slim blue shape materialised on a collision course with the little fish. Almost before Mike realised what was happening there was a sharp yank on the rod, followed by an easing of tension on the line. He reeled in the remaining few yards to find that only the tail stub of the mackerel remained on the hook. It would be nice to recount that he baited up again, before hooking and landing a 100 lb blue shark, but he never saw the fish again – his one and only encounter with the species.

Off the coast of Venezuela a charter boat was returning with three big marlin tied alongside, the product of ten hours of bluewater trolling. For much of the journey the mate, assisted by the two anglers, had been employed in repelling a group of sharks that were intent on dismembering the catch and had managed to mutilate the smallest billfish quite badly.

Very little in common between that story and Mike's encounter with the shark, you might think, but, believe it or not, the fish which nicked his bait could well have been one of the South American marlin-munchers. A bit far fetched? On the contrary, the results of tagging studies by biologist Dr. Stevens have shown some remarkable things about our sharks. Not least is the fact that, in the case of blue sharks at any rate, the activities of commercial fishermen and anglers off the coasts of Spain, Africa or even South America could have serious repercussions on our sport.

Most people think of sharks as fierce predators of anything (including themselves) that swims in the sea, but nothing could be further from the truth. In fact, many sharks are incredibly fussy about what they eat and some potential prey fish have capitalised on this. Certain soles, in particular, are not only distasteful to sharks but actively produce 'shark repellents'.

> **Certain soles actively produce 'shark repellents' and some may actually put sharks off their food.**

A fine tope. These powerful, hard-fighting sharks are fierce predators of bottom-feeding fish and travel long distances. This fish was returned, but not all tope are so fortunate. Captor: Jansen Teakle. Picture: Andy Evans.

These substances seem to be of two types: one which smells nasty to the sharks and the other an anti-feedant which actually puts the sharks off their food. Has anyone tried using soles for bait to see whether this works on other fish? We guess that they are too good on the dinner plate for that.

The presence of similar substances could partly explain why some fish are better baits than others. It occurs to us that wrasse, which sleep at night and would seem to be very vulnerable when dozing off, might also produce anti-feedant (possibly anti-conger) chemicals?

So what do sharks actually eat?

OK, so you never fish for *sharks*. Well, neither do we. Tope, however, are a different matter and are a popular sport fish all around the British Isles. In one study, 271 of these superb sporting fish, ranging from 10 lb to more than 50 lb, were tagged from angling catches. The tags were attached through little holes punched in the leading edge of the first dorsal fin. Over about ten years the tags from 42 of the tope were returned – roughly 14% of those released after capture. If we allow for the fact that some tags would have been lost and that quite a few of the tagged fish which were caught were probably not reported, a disturbingly high proportion of the tagged fish are being landed. In other words, they are already being heavily (over-)fished.

Tope tagged off the coast of England were returned from as far afield as Iceland and Spain. The longest period for which a tagged tope was at liberty was about 12 years and the greatest distance known to have been travelled was nearly 1,300 miles. The fastest tope covered, on average, at least two miles per day.

Tagging experiments also provide information on the growth rates of the tagged fish. It is now well known that tope grow rather slowly, with the smaller faster-growing fish gaining a meagre 3 in per year, while the big specimens increase less than 1 in in the same period of time, so a big tope must be very old.

What do tope eat? The Irish Sea study mentioned earlier showed that a wide variety of fish species made up 77% of the tope's food; a fair amount of the remainder was octopus (10%). Of the fish eaten, the most popular items were pouting/poor cod, mackerel, dragonet, herring and flatfish.

Blue sharks: long-distance specialists

Compared with the blue shark, the tope is a mere stay-at-home. Almost 2,600 blues were tagged in the above study and, of these, 51 were reported as having been caught again (only about 2%). One of these fish was not recaptured for almost 11 years and the seven most active sharks had travelled between (at least) 2,500 and 4,500 miles in their periods of freedom. Of course, it is likely that the fish had swum a great deal further than this, but there is no means of determining exactly how far. One shark tagged off southwest England was recovered in the Atlantic off South America.

Blue sharks are very active creatures and (as the crow flies) often move between one-and-a-half and four miles per day. They grow quite quickly and a decent-sized fish would normally gain about five inches in length every year.

A few porbeagles and makos were also caught and tagged and some of the tags were recovered. These oceanic sharks ranged from the cold waters of northern Norway to northern Spain, and one evaded recapture for as long as 13 years. The average growth rate of three tagged porbeagles was 10 in per year and that of a single mako less than half of this.

Sharks are by no means the only fish that are over-exploited. They share certain characteristics with some other species of fish that make them particularly susceptible to over-fishing. For example, species such as bass, which are slow-growing, long-lived and easily caught, can be quickly reduced to the state where big fish are scarce. In the 1970s, it was another of our small sharks, the spurdog, which suffered wholesale slaughter by commercial long-liners around the coast of Wales. Container loads of spurdogs, many in pup, were shipped across to the Continent because there was no domestic demand for them. When this sort of thing happens, from the angler's point of view at least, the prospect of catching anything other than the odd survivor becomes minimal and the stock recovery, if it comes

Many sharks migrate long distances.

about, can take many years. Tope, for example, mature at around 12 years of age and the females only reproduce every two to three years and then only have around 20 pups, many of which do not survive to breeding age.

In view of this and of the facts presented above, think very carefully next time you bring the graceful fawn-grey shape of a tope alongside your craft or when you first catch a glimpse of it in the beam of your headlamp. Try to practise what anglers should regard as the norm for these wonderful animals and carefully release your fish. In these days of simple digital photography there should be no need for anyone to feel that they must gloat over the smelly corpse of their prize. You will feel all the better for thinking that you, at least, are not contributing to the demise of the greatest sport in the world.

It is now mandatory for anglers to release all the tope they catch and that commercial fishermen landing tope bycatch into UK ports land the whole fish, rather than just the fins, which are by far the most valuable part of the animal. These measures were introduced by DEFRA in an effort to halt a hotly rumoured commercial tope finning fishery before it could get off the ground.

RAYS AND DOGFISH

It may be hard to believe, but snobbery is rife in sea angling circles. While most of us are happy to hook cod, conger, bass and plaice, we don't seem to get much joy when a lesser spotted dogfish or thornback ray snaffles our bait intended for something higher up the undersea social ladder. Why should this be? Is it simply the fact that many anglers believe that fish from the so-called primitive shark family, to which rays and dogfish belong, are inferior to those species with scales? We think not.

Bony fishes, that is to say all the scaly ones we normally regard as 'proper' fish, and members of the shark family (there are about 850 species of sharks, dogfish and rays alive today) parted ways roughly 460 million years ago, yet both groups have been great survivors in their own fashion. Each has produced its bottom-feeders, mid-water foragers and surface swimmers. The wide variety of flatfish ranging from tiny dab to mighty halibut is matched by designs that include small spotted rays and barn door skates. Even the sleek, fast-swimming tunas and bonitos have their shark-type equivalents in the streamlined porbeagle and mako sharks. Both of these groups tend to be warm-blooded.

Each of these two main groups of fishes has its own special features. Dogfish and rays are notable not just for their rough, prickly skins, porthole-like gill openings and multiple rows of teeth but also for their super-sensitive noses and educated electrical receivers. It is no accident that these fish can often find your bait on the darkest nights and in the murkiest water. The ability of that curse of a fish, the lesser spotted dog (LSD for short), to bite avidly when even the ubiquitous pouting have 'gone off' is well known to all.

German and American researchers have discovered that rays, scudding about on the sandy seabed, are even able to recognise their own kind by using high-tech transmissions. It seems that species such as our thornback, small-eyed and undulate rays, have electrical organs that are arranged in strips along each side of the tail. The output from these 'batteries' is much like the magnetic identity strip on your credit card.

Rays also have sensitive electricity detectors located in little jelly-filled pits in the skin. By setting up their own artificial electric organs buried under the sandy sea floor, scientists showed that not only did the rays find the transmitters and sit on top of them, but they often settled on the seabed piled on top of each other, resembling a skate sandwich.

It seems that when two of these fish first meet each other they send out friendly little impulses of electricity. The frequency and nature of the pulses vary from species to species. Conclusions drawn from these studies suggest that rays use electricity to signal to others of their kind, either warning them off their territories or perhaps using them for recognition during breeding. Skates and dogfish also use their detectors to locate food by means of the tiny outputs of electricity from the muscles of potential prey such as buried sandeels or flatfish.

> Rays are able to recognise other rays using their electrical sense.

When we first began fishing from small boats off the Dorset coast, many of the local anglers used to refer to all the different species of rays that they caught – thornback, small-eyed, blonde, spotted, undulate, the lot – simply as 'skate'. Although at that time we were not familiar with any of these fish and had never caught a 'flat-doggie', it was not long before we became fascinated and totally absorbed by the pursuit of them.

At first our attempts to catch them met with limited success, but even so it soon became obvious that a wide range of species was present over the mixed seabed around Swanage, Bournemouth and Weymouth. In depths of 3.5–9 m two species, small-eyed and spotted, were predominant on the widespread fine, firm, sandy ground.

Perhaps if we first of all describe our approach to catching these species along this coast, it will help to explain how they fit into the underwater scheme of things. The dinghy from which we fished was of marine-ply and fibreglass construction. It was an 11 ft, two/three-seater, one-man-power version propelled simply and more or less effectively by the combination of oars, back and arms. The seats were of painfully hard wood from which we shielded our backsides with chunks of foam rubber. These latter essentials were by far the most important items of equipment if we were to avoid medical complications (Farmer Giles/ Nobby Styles) from long sessions of ray fishing.

The dinghy would be rowed out into Swanage Bay and carefully positioned over one of the chosen marks, selected on the simple basis of previous results and by reference to various landmarks. Sometimes this positioning involved moving the anchor (a cold, wet business) three or four times to correct for subtleties of wind and tide. Of course, fish were probably present in lots of other places, but at least we had one less factor to worry about when we were analysing results.

Having achieved the correct spot to our satisfaction, one of us would sit in the stern, facing away from his rods but having the luxury of space to shuffle

Thornbacks, like this one,
eat lots of crabs.
Captor: Jansen Teakle.
Picture: Andy Evans.

his bum about. The other would occupy the tiny bow-seat, rather cramped but with a built-in backrest and the advantage of being able to see everything that was going on. If there were three in the boat the unlucky one would have the rowing seat with all the gear and no backrest at all.

In the dinghy tackle was carefully stowed (it had to be) so that it was: (a) ready to hand, (b) securely fastened and under cover from rain and spray, (c) placed on the curve of the hull to avoid slopping water from wet boots and anchor ropes. Bait boxes and the like were usually placed on the rower's seat amidships, so as to be within reach of both anglers. Each of us would fish two rods, one with 15-25 lb nylon monofilament line terminating in a wire trace (in case of conger) and with sufficient lead to anchor it firmly on the seabed. This rod was generally baited (at first) with the traditional and almost obligatory mackerel fillet.

The rod tip was set to project just beyond the gunnel and the reel put out of gear to allow a biting fish to take line against only the resistance of the ratchet without risk of the rod and reel arrowing over the side and into the depths (we never lost one).

The second rod was only a light spinning type with a simple nylon running ledger rig or paternoster, baited with worm or squid strip. This rod was held all the time to allow us to assess and react with reasonable speed to the bites of pouting, black bream or flatfish. Often the bites on worm-baited tackle were quite distinctive. There was the extremely faint pluck (try saying that after a few pints) of a dragonet or goby, the well-known and often-described rattling tug of small pouting or poor-cod, the strong lunging pull of a pollack and the even firmer knocks and yanks of black bream.

Quite often the ragworm was taken with a slow dragging draw, totally different from any of the others. The strike would be met with a solid resistance. There followed a sluggish, ponderous struggle in which the fish planed back and forth across the tide as it was gradually brought up to the boat. Depending on the colour of the water it would either be possible to see a yellow-brown disc in the depths or nothing at all until the fish broke surface.

The culprits were spotted rays which are possibly the most common shallow water species of ray off this part of the south coast. These fish never grow to any great size, with an average weight of only about 2–5 lb, but, on tackle intended for bream or pouting, they put up a pretty fair resistance. The most striking thing was that these fish nearly always took the ragworm baits, not the usual fish baits intended for their larger cousins. At first we put this down to the small size of the fish, but it makes even better sense when you look at a list of the food items eaten by spotted rays and recorded in scientific studies.

The diet of these rays varies a bit from place to place. For example, fish in Carmarthen Bay mostly eat crabs, while those in the Irish Sea rarely have these crustaceans in their stomachs. However, any angler with a serious desire to catch spotted rays should probably treat them as big flatties and leger with worm, shrimp or crab baits on light tackle over shallow, sandy seabeds. Spotted rays are very slow-growing fish, living up to 20 years, by which age they reach lengths of a little over 2 ft. Male and female fish grow at about the same rates.

Other common catches off the Dorset coast were small-eyed rays, which seemed to like the same sort of ground as their spotted relatives. Small-eyeds (in those days known as painted rays) almost invariably took our conger baits. Ten-pounders were not uncommon and the fish fought hard, even on our heavy gear, which was quite light by most boat-fishing standards. Unlike the spotted rays, small-eyed rays definitely preferred the fish baits to either crab or worm.

We have all seen pictures in the angling papers of groups of self-consciously smiling sea anglers surrounded by the glistening, angular white bodies of large catches of rays. Usually the fish in question are thornbacks and only the smiling mouths of their catch match the grins of the anglers. Somewhat to our surprise, our early efforts to catch rays from the dinghy rarely produced thornbacks. The thornback or roker, as it is also known, is a grand sea angler's fish. As we have said, this species was a fairly unusual catch over our normal fishing marks. Nevertheless, although much less common than in former times (over-fishing again), the thornback is still widespread around our coasts.

Catholic in its taste for food, on suitably light gear it is a hard-fighting and entertaining species. Many anglers must have heaved great sighs of relief when a long, cold session on beach or boat was saved by the intervention of a decent thornback. There is now plenty of information about this fish to give us a firm foundation on which to base our choice of angling methods. We would not presume to tell thornback experts what the best gear or tactics are (this must

The small-eyed ray, with its pale stripes, is much more of a fish eater than the thornback so baits such as sandeel and pouting are really effective for them. Picture: Andy Evans.

vary quite a bit with the area), but it is possible that, by taking a fresh look at the habits of the species, keen thornback anglers may be able to devise ways of improving their catches.

Consider first of all the nature of the fish. It is one of our largest rays, reaching weights of almost 40 lb in the case of big females. Despite this, most anglers consider a specimen of half that weight to be a hell of a fish, particularly in these times of over-fishing. The whole of the disc (the body and 'wings') is decorated with the large thorns from which the fish gets its popular name. The thorns are, in fact, enlarged denticles of the same type that make the skins of sharks and dogfish rough. The resemblance between the big thorns and the teeth of the thornback, which are also modified denticles, is very clear.

On the tails of both male and female fish some of the spines have massive knobbly bases. Those big spines are known as bucklers and large female thornbacks may even develop them on the underside, where they often become worn down by constant abrasion against the seabed. The upper surface of the thornback is camouflaged with a beautifully marbled combination of glistening grey-brown and creamy-white. Dark coloured eye spots, surrounded by smaller blackish dots, are often present and the younger, smaller individuals sometimes have a single large spot in the centre of each wing, which may occasionally lead to misidentification.

Both sexes become mature when they are between four and six years old and are about 2 ft in length. Each year, in the mating season, the claspers of the males increase in size and the cartilages within them develop into half-inch-long fearsome structures resembling hooks and razor blades that have to be seen (or felt) to be believed. In some cases, the claspers can be up to one-third of the fish length. From about April onwards the male thornbacks in Carmarthen Bay are fully developed, although one marine biologist, Holden, recorded a female with 'clasper wounds' (caused by the male's cartilages) as early as February, off Milford Haven.

Peak egg-laying takes place between May and September and each female thornback lays a pair of eggs (known as mermaid's purses) every two days, up to a total of 100 or more. Spawning females in laboratory tanks have been seen to seek out dark secluded corners in which to deposit their eggs. Each egg has a felt of sticky hairs on one side, which acts as a sort of Velcro, attaching them to sand grains, weed stems and rocks, reducing the chances of being disturbed or washed away.

Once they become mature the females breed every year. There seem to be roughly equal numbers of males and females, but the shoals of female fish (often bigger specimens than the males) migrate to the inshore spawning grounds in February to April and are only followed in by the males in April to June. Females live longer than the males; consequently most of the largest fish are females.

The results of scientific studies by marine researchers Ryland and Ajayi suggest that fishing pressure on thornback populations round our coasts is often greater than the stock can support and that numbers are rapidly declining. For example, Milford Haven commercial catches went down by about 25% between 1965 and 1971. No doubt there are far less fish by now, although, like many fish, rays have good year classes and poor ones. In view of the rather small number of eggs laid by the species, recovery from such a decline is likely to be very slow.

How does the thornback feed? As in other skates and rays, the protrusible mouth lies underneath the disc, which consists of wings and body, in the ideal position for picking up food items from the seabed without the fish having to change its normal swimming position. So that the ray can continue breathing without sucking in a mouthful of mud or sand, it draws water over the gills through holes (the spiracles) on the upper surface, just behind each eye. The water is then blown out through gill slits on the white under-surface.

The jaws of the fish are strongly muscled and well supplied with gripping, friction-pad-type teeth. Food is detected by sight, scent, movement and a well-developed electrical sense. Due to this versatile approach, prey can be captured both in daylight and in darkness or in deep and dirty water. Although most thornbacks are probably caught by anglers using fish baits, these rays are much less inclined to eat fish than many of their relatives. The main foods of thornbacks are various crustaceans. Shrimps, shore crabs, edible crabs, swimming crabs and even hermit crabs are consumed in large numbers. Very

Just behind the eye of rays such as this thornback is a hole or spiracle through which the fish breathes in. Picture: Chris Guest.

few molluscs or worms are eaten, apart from by the very youngest rays. Fish are only a small percentage of the roker's natural food.

Holden, Tucker and Ajayi have, between them, examined the digestive tracts of well over 1,000 thornbacks from around the coasts of England, Wales and Ireland. They showed that the food of the smaller fish is chiefly shrimps, which make up something like half the gut contents. The biggest thornbacks, those of most interest to anglers, eat mainly crabs, which comprise 70–80% of their diet. They do not seem to be fussy what sort of crabs they eat and the fish will swallow any crab which is common enough, slow enough and small enough to be captured and devoured. Perhaps here then (by our universal use of easy-to-procure fish baits) lies part of the reason for our early failures to catch many thornbacks in Swanage Bay.

Of course, thornbacks do sometimes eat fish and, as might be expected, the fish that are eaten are usually small, bottom-living types such as gobies, flatfish and the beautiful but very spiny dragonet – not that we often used any of these as bait. So there we have it, the logical approach to thornback fishing should involve the use of large crab baits or (very much second best) whole, live small fish such as gobies presented hard on the seabed and fished with a slow-retrieve technique. Common sense suggests that to avoid 'line bites' traces should be long enough to separate the bait by at least 3 ft or 4 ft from the lead and main line.

A good shore-caught female thornback. Thornbacks are pretty slow growers and only reach maturity when they are about 2 ft in length. Captor: Jansen Teakle. Picture: Andy Evans.

Preferred foods of sharks and rays

Thornbacks may be fussy about what they eat, but some members of the shark family, like the ubiquitous lesser spotted dogfish, are not exactly gourmets and will at times take almost any bait. Others, however, are quite fastidious. For example, the starry smoothhound (a fairly common catch these days) feeds almost exclusively on swimming crabs, while the monkfish (the shark relative, not the angler fish which fishmongers and TV chefs nowadays call 'monks'), now a pretty rare capture, devotes its life to devouring plaice, dabs, lemon sole and other flatfish.

On the subject of what these fish eat it may be worth mentioning a study carried out on some rays and dogfish in the Irish Sea. Most fish occasionally pick up a wide range of unusual food items so only the main foods will be mentioned:

- 73% of spotted ray food was crabs and shrimps and most of the remainder was worms. As mentioned above, the thornback also ate mostly crustaceans (80%).
- Blonde rays fed, to some extent, on shrimps, but more than half (52%) of their diet was sandeels.

The lesser spotted dogfish ate a huge range of different animals, including sponges, barnacles and sea anemones, but even here there were preferences. Hermit crabs weighed in at more than 20% (total crustaceans over half), worms were almost as popular (18%) and, despite their heavy protective shells, whelks were quite often preyed upon (3–4%).

Smoothhounds, like this one, are increasingly common around our shores. These hard-fighting little sharks feed largely on swimming crabs and other crustaceans. Captor: Chris Guest. Picture: Chris Guest.

Blonde rays live on similar ground to turbot and brill and, like them, feed heavily on sandeels and small fish. Captor: Clive Hodges. Picture: Kim Hodges.

A lesser spotted dogfish which has swallowed the hook, a good reason for giving circle hooks a try. Picture: Sea Angler magazine.

In another study, also in the Irish Sea, whelks and hermit crabs (usually living in whelk shells) were the main foods, particularly of larger dogfish. One curious and little-known fact (even by dogfish aficionados, if there are any) is that male dogfish have narrower mouths and snouts and longer teeth than females.

The migrations of lesser spotted dogfish have been traced, in the North Sea, by the use of acoustic tags. Sole were studied at the same time and, interestingly, it was found that while sole rested in the troughs between sand ridges, dogfish always settled on top of the ridges. It was also shown that both sole and dogfish are able to drift in mid-water, making use of the water currents to assist in their migrations, with one dogfish travelling up to ten miles in six hours.

> Rays and dogfish can find food by detecting tiny electrical muscle impulses from the prey.

The larger cousin of the lesser spotted dogfish, the bull huss (or greater spotted dogfish) eats octopus (23%), squat lobsters (15%) and crabs (15%).

Various studies have shown that spur dogfish (once a nuisance but now a rarity due to over-fishing) feed mainly on herring, sandeels and mackerel. Curiously, in the southern hemisphere (off New Zealand), the same species subsists almost entirely on swimming shrimps and crabs.

Where and when to fish

To return to the thornback, one viewpoint is to regard this as the least fussy of our rays. This lack of specialisation shows clearly in the wide variety of seabed types over which the species is caught. Silty mud, fine sand, grit, shell, stones and even rocky ground all produce their share of these fish.

Starting from scratch as thornback anglers, we would need to find out where, when and how to catch them. Where and when must be considered together because these fish, like most others, undertake yearly migrations for breeding and feeding. As mentioned already, thornbacks tend to swim about in groups, consisting of either male or female fish, for part of the year, although obviously the sexes must get together at some time.

A French scientist, Dr. Rousset, spent ten years tracking the distribution of rays and lesser spotted dogfish on the inshore fishing grounds of Brittany. The thornback ray was the most common and most widespread of the species examined in detail, seemingly because it was less fussy about the sort of seabed it lived on. Lesser spotted dogfish were also pretty common and, together with the thornbacks, made up two-thirds of the catch. Other less important species included small-eyed, spotted, blonde and undulate rays.

So just where should we seek out thornbacks? Rousset found that the majority of young rays and male rays (in other words, the smaller specimens) were found in the sheltered waters of the Bay of Douarnenez, while their larger mates and mothers were concentrated off more exposed stretches of coastline nearby. At times 80–100% of the fish from these latter areas were big females. Spawning took place between March and September, with the baby fish hatching four or five months after egg laying.

A bull huss – octopus is one of the favourite foods of these big dogfish. Captor: Jansen Teakle. Picture: Andy Evans.

Thornbacks tend to swim about in groups consisting of either male or female fish.

From February to April, 80–100% of thornbacks along the most exposed stretches of shoreline are big females.

Young thornbacks were about 6 in long. The infant fish grew quickly, reaching about 12 in within a year and about 18 in at two years of age. For older fish the picture of growth was a bit more confused, but they obviously attained a large size quite quickly off the French coast. Around our own shores it seems that thornbacks take longer to grow to a decent size and a big fish may be 10–15 years old.

The area from which Dr. Rousset's fish were caught is a large one, ranging in depth from a metre inshore to about 27 m near the outer edges of the bay. The inner, shallower areas are carpeted with fine sands and silts, while the deep water near the open sea is underlain by gravel and coarse sand.

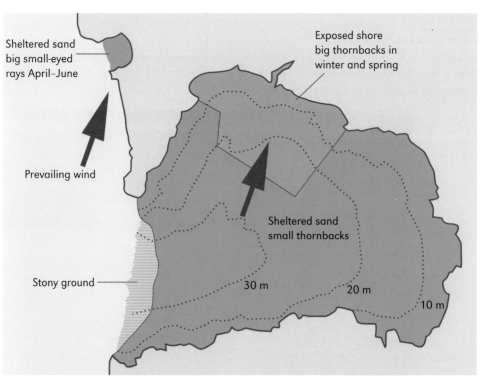

Sheltered sand
big small-eyed
rays April–June

Exposed shore
big thornbacks in
winter and spring

Prevailing wind

Sheltered sand
small thornbacks

Stony ground

30 m

20 m

10 m

The Bay of Douarnenez on the coast of Brittany, where rays are abundant. Big female thornbacks prefer the exposed shore in winter and spring, while small-eyed rays mostly inhabit the sheltered sediments of the smaller bay to the north.

Although the large female fish enter the exposed northern part of the bay in winter and leave in late spring, they often move quite close in along the sandy shore, which is exposed to the prevailing wind. Big fish never seemed to venture into the sheltered areas.

Large thornbacks avoid sheltered spots.

What about the other species? Small-eyed rays are scarce in the large bay but are even more abundant than the thornbacks in a much smaller cove further north along the coast,

Big small-eyed rays enter coarse sandy-bottomed areas between April and June. There is also an autumn influx of smaller immature fish.

the Bay of Bertheaume, which is floored entirely with coarse sand just like Swanage Bay. The big small-eyed rays enter the area to spawn and mate between April and June (the best time to catch them), to be followed by an autumn influx of smaller, immature specimens. These fish often associate with spotted rays and blonde rays, once again just as they do in our local bay at Swanage, in Dorset.

As often seems to happen, the observant angler's hunches, about where and when to find fish and what bait is best for a particular species, is borne out by scientific research, but sometimes the research sheds new light on the habits and preferences of our quarry and we risk missing new angling opportunities and improved catches if we ignore (or don't know about) the scientific information regarding our target species.

chapter_09

THE SCIENCE OF LURES AND BAITS
WELL WE NEVER KNEW THAT!

Fish senses: dim light vision

The June sun was now well above the horizon and, as Mike and his pals walked back along the shore, two other anglers approached from the cliff top field where they had parked the car. They halted briefly to exchange greetings and admired the two fine bass which Dave and Mike were carrying. The fish were the best of a catch they had made at daybreak and, like the ones that they had returned to the sea, were caught on spun lures. Their pre-breakfast return was because the fish had 'gone off' as the sun rose above the horizon.

A week or two earlier they had spent the afternoon and evening of a bright sunny day fishing from the steep rocky ledges of Seacombe. They had floated ragworm to take a few small pollack and wrasse, plus a single plump mackerel, which had grabbed the bait on the retrieve. All in all, it had been nothing to shout about. As the sun settled over the cliff top they decided to warm themselves up by spinning. It was a revelation! One pollack after another rocketed after the lures. Some were large by their usual rock-fishing standards and they landed at least two well in excess of 4 lb. All were returned to the water, but it was a treat to watch their muscular, bronze-olive shapes crashing, one after another, into the lures as the daylight faded from the sky.

Pollack, bass, scad, mackerel, coalfish, garfish and sea trout all feed and bite with exceptional ferocity in periods of changing light conditions. Why should this be?

Dawn and dusk. The change of light is a trigger for many predatory fish.

One of the leading authorities on this subject, Dr. Edmund Hobson, has frequently considered the question and it seems that what we anglers call 'pollack light' is definitely a matter of scientific fact. The reason why it pays to get out of bed before dawn or to hang on after your mates pack up their tackle in the evening are many and varied, but once they are pointed out the benefits are clear.

For a start, nearly all predatory sea fish depend on vision to direct their final attack on the sandeel, sprat, sand smelt or juvenile relative that takes their fancy. Because visibility in the sea is often poor (ask any diver), location of food, at distance, may depend chiefly on tastes, odours or vibrations carried by the water. However, in the final act of engulfing each victim, it is the sense of sight that matters most. This dependence on visible light gives us the first clue. However, if light is so useful to hunting predatory fish, why don't they all feed in the middle of the day?

For a start, the prey fish don't just sit about waiting to be eaten. If the attacking fish can see them, the prey are equally capable of seeing their aggressors. In daylight little fish will stray further and further from the weeds and rocks that provide their haven of refuge. The biggest specimens will wander further afield because their superior speed allows them to regain cover quicker than their smaller relatives when trouble appears over the horizon (or from

> Pollack, bass, scad, mackerel, coalfish, garfish and sea trout all feed and bite with exceptional ferocity in periods of changing light conditions.

behind a rock or clump of kelp). As evening approaches and the light begins to fail all the so-called 'forage fish' tend to beat a hasty retreat towards the nearest place of safety.

When the water is clear and undersea visibility is good, many small fish form schools in order to protect themselves. The reasons why it is safer to be a member of a school are many: early warning of danger by many pairs of eyes, the ability to confuse the attacker by presenting a much wider choice of victims and the ability to hide within a mass of similar fish, for example.

The appearance of a school of sandeels when they are illuminated by strong daylight clearly demonstrates yet another advantage. The predator is confronted by thousands of brilliantly flashing points of light, each one winking on and off as the prey fish twist and turn – a bedazzling experience for any sight-hunting animal. The weaving in and out of the little fish, combined with subtle effects of disruptive colour patterns, all add to the general confusion.

Hobson mentions that some predatory fish may have developed special tactics to overcome the problems of catching schooling fish in broad daylight. The bills of marlin, garfish and swordfish and the long tail of the thresher shark may be just such evolved gadgets. No doubt there are other ways round the problem that we have not yet recognised.

Nonetheless, it is a fact that many predatory fish accept the inevitable difficulties of catching prey unawares in the middle of bright sunny days when the water is crystal clear. In these conditions the predators are very visible and simply do not feed. Sometimes they will, of course, be lucky and come upon an unfortunate little fish which has strayed too far from its refuge, but, more often, it pays them to save their energy and the wise angler should do the same and fish for something else.

> It is critical to be there and fishing when the big fish have their daily feast.

At the other end of the scale are the hours of darkness. It is obvious that under these conditions fish must depend on being able to sense vibrations or chemical secretions of their potential victims and only a few of them are equipped well enough to catch fast-swimming, elusive prey.

So, only the rather brief periods of dusk and dawn remain for predators to gain the upper hand. As the night shift of small foragers changes over to the daytime feeders, the bass, pollack, cod, coalfish and sea trout take their chance. What sort of things could give them the edge over their potential food? Large eyes collect every photon of light enabling them to pick out the most vulnerable specimens – those which have become separated from their fellows or which behave in an unusual fashion. In the tropics, where night falls suddenly, these feeding periods will be very short, perhaps as little as 20 minutes. Here in Britain, it can often be rather longer, but even so it is clearly critical to be there and fishing when the big fish have their daily feast.

Perhaps the most important aspect of dawn and dusk underwater is the low angle presented by sunlight falling on the water surface. This means that only a little light penetrates the depths to illuminate the camouflage-and-confuse systems of small forage fish (or, presumably, the outline of the attacking predator). In contrast, there is still plenty of background (sky) light to silhouette the outlines of prey to predators attacking from below. Bass and pollack are well aware of the advantage this gives them and they direct their attacks accordingly.

Anyone who reads angling books and articles in magazines must be familiar with the adage: wait until the day-trippers have left the beaches before venturing out. Holidaymakers or no, it will often be the early (or late) angler that catches the fish.

Fish senses: the sweet smell of success

'When the water is dirty after a storm it's best to use a big, smelly bait like a whole squid, half a dozen lugworm or a big peeler crab.' 'When fish are finicky the flash of lures made from Mylar or a bright silver spoon will attract mackerel better than an old-fashioned set of feathers.' 'In matches I always tip my baits with white rag/a crab leg and there is no doubt that it improves catches.' How often have you heard an angler say something like this or read similar comments in the angling press? Some of these statements have more than a grain of truth in them, but sea anglers and writers are only too ready to present their ideas, however dubious they may be, as hard facts. However, Mr Average Angler is not quite as gullible as he or she might seem and discussions in the club house, on the shore or at the bar often centre around the latest flight of fancy from an over-confident columnist. It all boils down to fish senses and just what they are able to see, smell, taste and feel. There is quite a lot known about the way in which sea fish find their prey and we have written about it on more than one occasion.

To give just a couple of examples: cod tend to hunt at night or in dirty water by swimming downtide and 'sniffing' for prey. Having detected a scent they do a U-turn and track it uptide before finally locating the lugworm, fish or crab by sight or by means of their chin barbel or pelvic fins, which are sensitive organs of taste. A second case study showed that sight-feeding flatfish respond in different ways to the shapes of their prey. Turbot are attracted to the long thin form of sandeels and actively avoid large lumps of lead dangling in front of them. Dogfish and rays use the tiny electrical signals given off by buried flatfish to help them detect their prey.

Very often the true facts about how fish find, recognise and attack their potential food are hidden in obscure scientific journals. There is no way that we could all keep track of such information and, even if we were able to, it would be no easy matter to translate it into better fishing methods.

> Sole are just as good at feeding at night-time or in dirty water as in daylight. Plaice, on the other hand, feed mainly in the daytime.

> At night or in dirty water, cod and whiting both locate their food largely by the chemicals that ooze from it.

A pollack showing the nostrils (or nares) just in front of the eye. Water goes in the front opening and out of the other.

Certainly, the academics are not going to tell us how to catch fish. It is up to us to devise ways of putting these facts to good use. No single person has a monopoly of good ideas and, indeed, it would be impossible for anyone, on their own, to try out new baits, tackles or methods effectively (whatever bait and tackle salesmen might suggest in their adverts).

To get down to the latest information, fish make the most of all their available senses to maximise the efficiency of their feeding behaviour, but the dominance of vision, scent or taste often changes as the fish grows. Take a simple example: almost all baby fish, drifting in the plankton, are sight feeders and only switch to other methods as they get older. Adult fish of several species may forage over the same ground, but each will use different tactics or will have a body adapted to avoid too much competition for the same food. The principle is similar to the differences in beak length and shape in wading birds. Clearly the curlew with its long curved beak is designed to dig deeper than the beakily challenged redshank or sanderling and so on.

Are 'superbaits' a possibility?

Some 50-odd years ago Mike spent the whole of one summer working as a student at the research laboratories of the Marine Biological Association. The labs are situated on Citadel Hill and overlook the waters of Plymouth Sound, sheltered by a huge stone breakwater, and (in those days at least) the area was teeming with fish. Most of his evenings were spent fishing from the local rocks and jetties and, as he remembers it, the weather was perpetually sunny and warm.

That summer was notable in two respects. Firstly for the episode in which Mike accidentally blocked the lavatories of the YMCA where he lodged during his stay with an enormous parcel of 'surplus to requirements' squid, which refused to flush away, and for subsequently spending the entire evening up to his armpits down the pan trying to remove the offending molluscs from the U-bend. Secondly, and more pertinently, were the many hours of mackerel fishing. The method he used varied a little with the wind, time and tide conditions, but by far the most interesting sport was obtained by light-float fishing from the breakwater arms.

Mike's teacher, Les, was an angler who worked at the laboratories. He showed Mike how to set up his favourite sliding-float gear and told him how the best depth at which to fish varied from 5 ft to 20 ft (1.5–6 m), shallower in good weather. Les also demonstrated the art of catching the 'brit' that they used for bait. Although the brit (whitebait) were often abundant near the water surface, they were distinctly nippy and difficult to catch. The only way in which it was possible to obtain decent numbers of the little silver fish was by using a large dip net on a stout pole.

To build up enough speed in the head of the net it was slashed into the water, edge on, and then twisted through 90 degrees to catch the brit. Mike kept his baits in an old plastic maggot box and Les kept his in a small tobacco tin. Their tackle was almost identical and the fine wire hooks were baited with small bunches of two or three dead fish hooked through the heads. Despite the fact that Mike was eager to learn and slavishly copied the master's tactics, Les, almost always, had about twice as many bites and fish as Mike.

It was only after several weeks of friendly competition that Les let Mike into his secret. In his tackle box he carried a small bottle of pilchard oil with which, before each trip, he would anoint the interior of his little bait tin. Now, in view of the fact that the mackerel is basically a sight feeder, using its large and efficient eyes to find and recognise its prey, we are not sure whether oiled baits really made the difference between their catches, but Mike began to use oil and gradually his take improved. Possibly the improvement was simply a result of increasing skill with the method, but it was Mike's first inkling that bait additives might have a place in sea angling.

Additives such as aniseed, custard powder and sugar have been mixed with bread paste and used in freshwater fishing for many years. Nowadays amino acids, peptides, polypeptides, proteins and a wide range of other compounds and flavours are sold to anglers and added to their baits in the belief that carp, in particular, will find them distinctive, attractive or stimulating. Some are even claimed to be irresistible.

It is logical that fish feeding mostly by the use of their scent and/or taste capabilities on highly specialised diets should be well able to identify and locate substances given off by their preferred food. In much the same way that we are attracted (and our hunger is increased) by the smells wafting from the ventilator of the fish and chip shop or from the oven door when the Sunday joint is cooking (can anyone still remember Sunday joints?), so the carp may detect buried midge larvae or worms by traces of moulting fluid or excretory waste leaking into the water.

There is no doubt that the sort of effect which we describe is real and worthwhile to the fish-catcher because for some years the hunt for artificially flavoured crab, lobster and tuna baits has been gathering momentum in the scientific world. There is now quite a lot of evidence that both freshwater and marine fish use the 'key substance' approach to food location and identification.

In the original *Operation Sea Angler*, Mike described how it was discovered that cod locate their prey by means of scent trails, the fish turning up-current and searching for the source of squid juice released from a tiny pipe into the flowing sea water. This cod study was conducted by Dr. Mike Pawson, of the former Ministry of Agriculture, Fisheries and Food. Pawson also tried to identify the attractive chemicals, extracted from lugworms, in a tank experiment. The fish used were whiting and cod. It was already known that, at night or in dirty water, both species locate their food largely by the chemicals that ooze from it. To test the reactions of the fish to natural attractants a specially designed tank was set up. Food extract was introduced at one or other of the inflow pipes and the behaviour of the cod or whiting in the middle part of the tank was observed. The activities of the fish were classified according to the amount of interest that they showed in the extracts more or less as follows:

1 No interest or response
2 Aware of presence
3 Feeble searching
4 Persistent searching
5 Searching, backing up and biting at the food pipe
6 Directed searching, backing and biting at the pipe.

The fish were tested first for their reactions to plain sea water flowing from the food pipes. Invariably, it was totally ignored. Whole extracts of lugworm, ragworm, mussel and squid were prepared in a blender and the bits and solids were filtered off before the tests. Various individual chemicals separated from the lugworm extract were also used for tests.

For most of the time the cod and whiting remained swimming about in the central part of the tank in mid-water with their thin pelvic fins (feelers) tucked tightly against the body. When they were disturbed or frightened they swam near the bottom or walls of the tank, their fins were all laid flat and a patchy camouflage pattern developed on the backs of the fish. Both species noticed bits of food moving in mid-water, but whiting, in particular, did not seem to be aware of food lying still on the bottom of the tank. In contrast, cod occasionally went straight to such items and ate them whole.

Both cod and whiting reacted to the presence of all four bait smells by going to the bottom of the tank, extending the pelvic feelers downwards to contact the bed and by swimming faster. They were well aware of the presence of the chemical cocktail and responded even without knowing where it was coming from. After becoming aware, the fish began to search by swimming along and trailing their 'antennae' on the bottom of the tank. They twisted and turned back and forth until they found the opening of the food pipe.

If the trailing fins touched a piece of food the fish backed up and ate it or, if it was buried, they dug it up, rejecting the inedible particles of sand or gravel. All four bait extracts produced the same sort of behaviour. Some of the separate chemicals from the liquidised lugworm gave a similar response to whole bait juices and the active portion seemed to include seven amino acids. The amino acids serine and glycine produced grade 4 responses (as listed above) even at very low concentrations.

Whiting failed to respond to any mixture of amino acids if glycine and alanine were not present. Several other amino acids (arginine, taurine, aspartine and cysteine) gave only the very lowest level (grade 1) responses.

At extremely low concentrations of bait extract the fish were unable to find the source of the attractant, even though their behaviour showed that they knew it was there. Mixtures of amino acids generally produced stronger responses than individual compounds, showing that no single substance was the perfect attractant. Although for cod and whiting glycine seemed to be the basis of attraction, it was still less effective than natural lugworm, so other substances are certainly involved.

This account shows that we are only scratching the surface of the possibilities suggested by our meagre knowledge of bait additives. Elsewhere Mike has described the use of amino acids as a feeding stimulant for sole and many anglers have commented on the pulling power of baits such as peeler crab. Surely the not-too-distant future will see the development of concentrated 'super baits' in the field of commercial fishing and we should not be afraid to follow the lead of the professionals. Until then, it seems that there is nothing to beat a bit of fresh natural bait, although, as we write this book, the latest soft plastic lures, which are becoming popular with sea anglers, are often impregnated with artificial scents or come packed in 'juices', which some claim boost their catch rates. The jury is still out as far as we are concerned, but we keep an open mind and watch developments with interest.

> Although science has identified both chemical attractants and feeding stimulants, there is still nothing to beat a bit of fresh natural bait.

Before we finish on this subject there is just one other thing worth a mention. In addition to the observations on fish there is also a well-documented phenomenon of chemical attraction in marine invertebrates and a wide range of avoidance reactions has been recorded. Various scientific and other observations seem to support the idea that the dead remains of certain crustaceans may repel live animals of the same species. In particular, field experiments are reported in which the catches of an Australian rock lobster were greatly reduced by including bits of dead rock lobster with the bait normally used in the traps. It was concluded that the most effective artificial bait would be one which involves not only attraction of the species that you want to catch, but also something that repels the ones you don't want.

The chemical basis for this is probably apparent from reactions that are commonly known. So what? you might say. But if live crabs can be repelled by the smell of dead crabs – is it possible, for example, that a portion of dead shore crab attached to the hook could protect your bait from the depredations of living shore crabs? This could be a real bonus.

> A portion of dead shore crab attached to the hook could protect your bait from the depredations of living shore crabs.

Artificial baits: why bother?

When we discuss lure fishing with other anglers they frequently express concern at the possibility of losing fish (or lures). The usual comment is that they would not like to think of a fish swimming round with its mouth sealed by a treble hook. Obviously this can happen, but it is rather rare to lose any fish at all if suitable tackle and tactics are used.

We will assume that the tackle used for deep-water pirking or jigging is generally hefty enough to avoid breakage, except when you foul the seabed or a chunk of wreck superstructure. It is also not worth worrying about anyone who uses silly tackle in the hunt for line class records or cash. If the rod and reel are suited to fish and fishing conditions, if line strength is reasonable and if the angler ties a decent knot and checks his line for cuts and nicks, the only weaknesses may be swivels, split rings and the hooks themselves.

Most lures work best when they are unhampered by stiff lines or big swivels. Fortunately, even the smallest modern swivels are generally strong enough for conventional spinning tactics. The same is not true of split links and clips.

The design of some clips leaves much to be desired, but, apart from that, many of them are subject to metal fatigue after a session involving a number of lure changes. All links lose their elasticity and become unreliable when they are affected by corrosion, so if you must use them change them frequently. We rarely use links of any description these days, preferring to tie a non-slip loop knot in the nylon trace or, when toothy fish are present, in the knottable wire leader.

Lure hooks also present a number of problems. However, the principles should be the same as for bait fishing: hooks should be sharp, fine in the wire, short in the point and with barbs as small and neat as possible. On some lures, such as the original Redgills, the large hooks provided to fit the lure and give weight are far coarser than is necessary to land any fish that swims. It needs little ingenuity to change the hooks for more suitable ones while still retaining the balance and action of the lure. It is always worth flattening coarse barbs by using a pair of pliers because they rarely come unstuck but, when modified, are much easier to remove by hand (or for that matter from the hand – we know, we've done it).

Spoons, spinners (such as Mepps) and plugs are usually armed with trebles of varying quality. If necessary, replace them with good trebles or, if it is appropriate and you prefer it, with singles. Some plugs can't be fitted with conventional single hooks because of the position of the eye so, if you are really concerned, there is nothing to stop you cutting the two least effective points from the treble. If the resulting loss of weight affects the action of the lure, add a little lead wire to the hook shank or replace the hook with one a size or two larger.

Artificial baits: lure colour

You are out for a wrecking session in mid-Channel. It is a beautiful day with only a slight chop on the water. Everyone in the boat is armed with similar gear, boat rods, multipliers, flying collar rigs and plastic eels. The only real difference is the colour of the eels and everyone has their favourite. You have decided to stick to the orange-tailed black 'Afterburner' which has served you well in the past. On the first drift your pal, in the stern, using a plain red eel hits a decent pollack, but everyone else goes without a bite. Another drift and again your mate has a good fish. Jammy so and so! After the third time over the mark when the luck once more goes to the Redgill everyone is rummaging in their tackle boxes for a suitably rosy replica of the successful lure. Could it be that the colour of the lure makes a difference or is it just some subtlety of tactics or perhaps simply luck? You may never know, but is it possible to find out?

Mike often uses small plastic eels instead of flies when he is fly fishing for pollack, mackerel and bass. Usually he fishes at first light and the eels, for simplicity, are either black or white. He also wondered whether colour made a difference. Now he admits that he is no great fly caster. He says that he simply uses fly tackle for amusement, even though he knows that it would often be possible for him to catch many more (and probably larger) fish on plugs or spoons. Most of the fish that he catches on the fly need only a moderate cast and many of them are only a few yards beyond the rod tip.

For this fly dabbling, Mike's favourite lure is a tiny Redgill or Delta-type eel and as an experiment on a couple of occasions he tried two flies, a 'natural' (silvery-white) one on the point and a black one about a foot up the cast. The idea was not to catch two fish at once but to see whether the colour of the fly made any difference.

On the first session he had fish on both flies, but after the third mackerel a garfish grabbed the black fly and (unknown to Mike) damaged the nylon so badly that the next bite took the black fly off. He was too lazy to replace it so the experiment ended prematurely. On the next session, the first six mackerel were all on the white lure, the seventh and eighth were one on each (at the same time) and the ninth (presumably another garfish) nicked the black fly clean off, once more with hardly a tug. He resolved to try again with the black one on as the 'point fly' next time.

The idea, as we said, was not to catch fish two at a time but to compare the effectiveness of the two contrasting lure colours. The thought of trying it came to Mike when he realised that he could catch four or five species, on fly, from one spot, hopefully in sufficient numbers to make the experiment worthwhile.

Later that year, when there were more fish about, he tried to improve his approach. The gear was a trout fly rod with a number seven, weight forward, floating line. On the end of the line was a length of 6 lb nylon with a dropper tied part way along. A couple of 3 in eels were attached, one black and one white, and when he was catching fish he simply kept a count in his head of the number and species caught on each. Sometimes the action was almost too thick and fast to keep a true count, but the numbers are just about right. Of course, with two flies it quite often happens that two fish are landed at once and it can be a bit tricky to know which fly was taken first so this distorts the picture somewhat.

Normally fishing starts before it gets light and typically the fish don't begin to bite for perhaps ten minutes after the first cast. On Mike's first attempt he had three pollack and a scad on the black fly and one pollack on the white fly – interesting. It then blew up for a few days and he did not fish. Next trip was a bit more productive and he landed four pollack and five mackerel on the black and two pollack, two garfish (one black, one white), a bass and 18 mackerel on the white fly – conclusive you might think. Next trip, however, he had 24 pollack in more or less equal numbers on the black and white flies, two scad (one on black, one on white) and two mackerel (one on black, one on white). All in all, it did not seem to prove anything much, with the different species taking both colours. The totals were:

- Pollack: 19 black/15 white;
- Scad: 2 black/1 white;
- Mackerel: 6 black/19 white (the only significant difference in colour preference);
- Garfish:1 black/1 white
- Bass: 1 white.

Of course, the real interest was not in which species took which fly, but in the fact that most of the pollack and scad were caught early in the session when it was darker and most of the mackerel and garfish later in the session when it was lighter. Perhaps (just perhaps at the moment) the black fly was a bit more productive in the gloom and the white fly in the daylight. What is really needed is two anglers fishing side by side, at the same time, with different-coloured flies and using the same simple technique (more whipping the water than fly casting). Ideally there should be a third hardy soul not fishing but recording the results. (Mike's wife, who loves data, says that if she could get out of bed she could do this.)

It should be mentioned that the fish were feeding on sprats about the same size or a bit bigger than the flies. Incidentally, on the last trip Mike changed his cast from nylon to a fast-sinking braid – he says that he is sure it did not affect the species of fish caught (the mackerel were thin on the ground and the pollack prolific) – but it seemed to enhance the proportion of hooked bites.

The experiment was simply to compare black and white flies (plastic eels) as they were fished through the change of light at dawn. The following season Mike decided to repeat the experiment (always a mistake). To cut a long story short, this time all the fish took the white lure, even when it was still very dark. Rarely are these things cut and dried when it comes down to it. Of course, in most cases you are only fishing with a single lure so it is very difficult to do any sort of comparison or control on your tactics. If there are two of you fishing you can each use a different lure, but no two anglers ever fish in exactly the same way. Even with the 'black and white' experiment the position of the fly on the cast may have had an effect (whether it is on the point or the dropper).

In truth, we should really keep up the experiment, try the test time after time and then do some statistics on the results, but life, as they say, is too short. We don't really want to spend a whole summer fishing for mackerel and small pollack, entertaining though it is. The outcome of this fiddling about is to make us even more sceptical (if that's possible) of many claims such as 'red-eyed chartreuse blue-spotted shads are the only lure for coalfish over wrecks', etc.

So are there any solid facts concerning the effectiveness of different coloured lures which might throw some light on the subject? It seems that there are a few.

Scientists have compared the catch rates of some sea fish when using artificial lures in an automated hand-line fishery off the Shetland Islands. First a few words about this commercial jigging or automated hand-lining tactic. The reasoning behind this study was that although different types and colours of artificial lures are widely available to commercial fishermen, there is not much information about whether a particular design of lure worked best or whether something as simple as lure colour affected catches (just what we'd like to know, of course). Catch rates were compared for five different colours of rubber tube lures and for five different designs of artificial lure commonly used in hand-line fisheries.

The lures are jigged up and down in the water. Jig fishing tactics have been used for centuries by fishermen in the North Sea and North Atlantic and many of the techniques are still in use today. In recent years, however, hydraulic or electric automatic jigging machines have been introduced to make it easier to haul fish up from the depths. The machines can be programmed to change the jigging pattern and a pilot study was carried out in the inshore waters around Shetland.

Most of the fishing took place over rough, untrawlable bottoms such as hard ground, areas of rocky peaks on the sea floor and wrecks. During fishing the vessel was drifted over the fishing ground with the engine switched off. If the fishing was poor during the drift the vessel moved to a different area. Almost 500 hours were spent actively fishing various places over a 15-month period. Not surprisingly, wrecks produced the greatest amount of fish, followed by rocky peaks and hard ground in third place. Pollack and coalfish made up most of the catch, 54% and 37% respectively. Smaller numbers of cod (3%) and ling (5%) were also caught.

The factor that had the most effect on catches was tide. In many places fish would suddenly stop biting when the tide changed (did they move or did they stop feeding? – see chapter 7). However, at some other marks there was

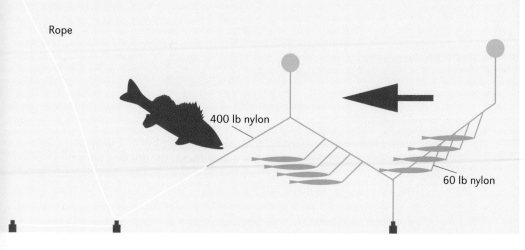

Rope

400 lb nylon

60 lb nylon

Long-lines set with lures can be effective for catching bass. In contrast to the use of nets the by-catch on lures is negligible.

no clear relationship between tide and catch rates. Wind speed and direction, daylight patterns and weather conditions also had lesser effects on catch rates. The most successful method of catching pollack was jigging the artificial lures close to the seabed. It was not clear whether coalfish were permanently resident on particular wrecks, whether they moved between wrecks or if, at times, they migrated away from the area altogether.

The important finding for us is that lure colour made no difference to catches of pollack, coalfish, cod or ling. The only positive result was that cod did seem to prefer the lower hooks (there were six hooks on each line) when lures were black. Pollack, in contrast, were more attracted to the lower hooks when the lures were coloured blue. The type of lure also made no difference to catches of coalfish, cod or ling. However, catches of pollack on a novel 'sonar' lure were poorer than on any of the others. It did not seem to make any difference where any of the lures were positioned along the line.

> Lure colour made no difference to catches of pollack, coalfish, cod or ling.

The only other worthwhile study of lure fishing we could find was related to using lures on set long-lines for bass. The system, using monofilament lines and artificial lures, was developed in response to the rise in consumer demand for line-caught bass. Unlike nets, it would allow commercial fishermen (they claim) to target bass without much impact on the wider environment. They would also be able to fish in waters with tricky tidal conditions or legal restrictions on the use of nets. The study involved a six-month trial from May to October off the coast of North Devon.

Apart from catching bass to sell, the idea was to reduce the need for livebait and to allow fishing in waters where netting was restricted or difficult. The method (just like angling) should also minimise by-catch and reduce the catch of undersized fish. Since there was no need to rebait, the lines could be fished for up to two weeks continuously, being harvested daily. Fishermen would be able to take full advantage of favourable conditions, having gear set up and ready to go at all times.

The idea is that the monofilament long-lines are suspended between the surface and seabed. From these lines artificial lures are attached at equal distances. The lines can be left in place for long periods and actively fish all the time. Expensive lures would be out of the question for commercial use so low-cost, easily made gear was the order of the day. The main line ranged from 400 lb down to 200 lb breaking strain. Durable Berkley swivels were the best as other types deteriorated quickly (we have used Berkley swivels for years). Aluminium or stainless steel-coated double crimps, in conjunction with plastic sleeves, were used to hold the swivels in position on the main line. This eliminated the swivel chafing through the heavy line. Small rubber 'lamb's rings' were tied in to the droppers to act as shock absorbers and to avoid the fish running and snapping the line when hooked (shades of 'pole elastic').

Due to continual immersion, corrosion quickly rendered cheap hooks useless so stainless steel or Duratin was essential. The best hook size varied with the size of fish being caught but ranged from 3/0 to 5/0. Hooks were snelled (whipped on), rather than tied, to avoid fish chafing through knots. Snoods (droppers) were of 60 lb breaking strain monofilament (pretty hefty by rod and line lure angling standards). The best length for the snood, to allow the maximum number to be deployed on a line, was 5 ft (1.5 m). Interestingly, a luminescent bead on the end of the snood (at the head of the lure) seemed to increase the catch rate.

As in the jigging experiments, tide was very important and a current of at least 0.8 knots was needed to keep the lures working. Above 3 knots the lures began to spin and this reduced their effectiveness. It was noted that bass moved about to feed in an optimal tidal flow which fell between the 0.8 and 3 knot current speeds.

At first, lines were shot across the tide to allow the lures and snood to be held well away from the back line. However, fish were found to be running uptide in quite narrow bands, resulting in the catch being distributed in isolated patches rather than along the whole line. With the lines running across the tide, the hooks were also prone to catch far more rubbish (weed, plastics etc.), which in extreme cases would chafe through the back line. Consequently the lines were later set along the direction of flow.

The colour of the water was a consideration; both too clear and too dirty were worse than something in between. Very high turbidity (visibility less than 3 ft) and very clear water (visibility more than 24 ft) caused big reductions in catch. Vibration, it was thought, could have helped fish to find lures in murky water. In gin-clear conditions, it was considered that fish were mostly caught at the change of light, around dawn and dusk (confirming our preferences).

The best visibility for fishing was found to be between 9 ft and 15 ft. Of course, anglers using finer, less visible gear and more realistic lures may do rather better in clear water conditions.

Scent was experimented with as an added attractant. Amazingly, when lures were dressed in pilchard oil prior to fishing it reduced catches. While the lures had traces of oil on them, they did not catch bass. It is not known if other attractants might work. However, the lures fished well without scent in all but the dirtiest water. May bloom and any other algal infestation rendered the lines as good as useless and rubbish catching on the lines spoiled their effectiveness.

> **Lures that had traces of pilchard oil on them did not catch bass.**

The lines were fished in some areas notorious for seals damaging fishing gear and catches. There were incidences of hooked pollack being eaten by seals while bass on the adjacent hook were alive and untouched. There were no incidences of half-eaten bass, but when seals were present in the vicinity, catches decreased.

The catch data was based on bass caught per number of hooks each day. In the early days only a small number of lures (60–180) were used at a time. This was while the lines were being tested to eliminate problems. Later, as the lines were modified with experience, more bass were caught for a given number of lures set. Part of this improvement must have been due to the increasing numbers of fish available as the season progressed. When properly set, the lines caught one bass per 12 lures. The majority of the fish caught were bass. By-catch made up only a tiny percentage of the overall catch. Pollack were the most common 'other fish', along with cod. Species other than bass were, in most cases, returned alive.

During the early trials there were two gannets and three herring gulls caught by accident. Later, with the lines set better, there were no incidents of bird by-catch, even though gannets were seen working in the area during the course of the later trials.

So there we have it. All the observations should probably be taken with a large pinch of salt (water), but what can we, as lure anglers, conclude from these tests?

- Firstly, lure colour may not make much difference to effectiveness, but a spot of luminescence on the trace could help induce bites.
- In murky waters a lure with plenty of vibration may improve results.
- Lures can be effective even when tied to pretty hefty nylon lines, but in very clear water it could be worth refining the tackle a bit.
- Scenting lures may, in some cases, put fish off.
- Bass run uptide in quite narrow lanes, so try to fish across the flow until you locate them and then fish at the same distance where you had your bite.
- Bass will take lures fished slowly against the flow pretty well.

chapter_**10**

WHAT'S YOUR LINE?
AND THE REEL
TO HOLD IT

LINES

The fight

The pebbles clicked and rattled beneath our rubber-booted feet as we crossed the ridge of the great gravel beach. Our breath condensed into white smoke in the chill air as we set up the rusty monopods and then lobbed generous chunks of squid into the rolling grey winter sea. It was a good evening and the bites came hard and fast. We were kept busy with a succession of codling and big whiting. The tip of the beach caster knocked smartly to the pull of a hungry fish and, if the strike was firm and effective, two, three, four or five pounds of muscular fish would be pumped swiftly ashore. The clutch on one or other of our reels would occasionally yield a bit of line on the strike and, on one occasion, the best cod of the day dragged off 10 ft or 12 ft of 15 lb line, against heavy pressure, as the fish was swept out to sea by the strong undertow.

Contrast the above description of one of our better beach-casting sessions with the following account taken from the original *Operation Sea Angler*.

The rod of one angler bent double and the ratchet screamed as 30 yards of line were torn off in a few seconds. He stumbled over the hummocks of decaying wrack and the breaking waves surged up his bare legs as, rod held high, he followed the course of the hooked fish along the beach. Fragments of weed flew in all directions as the fish again sped out to sea. In the ensuing battle angler and mullet alternately gained control, but gradually, under the relentless pressure of 6 lb line, the fish began to tire. Five minutes later a 4 lb mullet was drawn over the rim of the large net.

Both accounts are, as near as we can describe, accurate. Both trips produced the sort of enjoyment and satisfaction that only a sea angler would experience. The fish were about the same size, the sea conditions were similar, but clearly the battles with the hooked fish were complete contrasts. Cod and grey mullet differ a good deal in their appearance and build, but both have to feed and live in strong currents, heaving seas and rugged terrain, so their swimming capabilities are probably not very different.

The main differences between the sessions relate to the tackle used. In both cases the gear would be regarded by most anglers as appropriate to the situation. The codling were taken on 15 lb line armed with 3/0 hooks and anchored by a few ounces of lead, while the mullet was beaten on a 6 lb nylon monofilament cast, #7 floating fly line and size 12 hook adorned with a tiny imitation maggot fly. There is no doubt that if the fish and tackles were reversed the tussles would not have been very different and that the codling might have been just as awkward to land as the thick-lipped mullet.

Wherever you fish in lake, river or sea and whether your quarry is shark, plaice, skate or silver eel, the same principles apply. Given plenty of open, snag-free water and a hook length or trace which will withstand the chomping of toothy jaws (or rubbery lips in the case of mullet), the line used simply needs to be strong enough to turn a fish before it empties your reel. By now we expect that some sea anglers reading this will have labelled us as light tackle cranks. In fact, anyone who knows us could confirm that, if anything, the reverse is true.

When Mike was a youngster living in Leeds, he coarse-fished using traditional fine lines and float tackle, often struggling to catch anything at all. Then, when he was 13 he saw the light. The angling guru of his teenage years was the late Richard Walker, who revealed all in the pages of his book *Still Water Angling*. From then on, not for Mike the 2 lb line and size 16 hook for carp. Even the good old roach was (and still is occasionally) sought with number 6 or 8 hooks baited with small golf balls of bread. The key theme of Walker's book, you see, was the use of suitable tackle to match the fish and the conditions. Mike was an instant convert.

Some twenty years later, Steve (the young whippersnapper) also discovered Walker's writings and drew the same inspiration from those pages. It was not for another decade though that our paths would cross and lead us to share many ideas and angling adventures of our own. Since those early days we have indulged in most forms of angling. We still have blank sessions and still occasionally lose fish for a variety of reasons. When our line goes slack after an unmissable bite or a brief tussle with an unseen adversary we still feel that same dreadful sense of loss. However, we can scarcely remember losing a fish because the line was too weak.

Light lines and small hooks, properly handled, are capable of landing very large fish.

Usually the fish escaped because we had failed to anticipate a potential hazard and were unable to react quickly enough when an emergency arose. For example, one of the last fish to obtain its freedom in this way (a few years ago now) was a bass of about 8 lb. Having played the fish for some

The 'danger periods' are when fish shoot away from a standing start, when you try to stop them dead on a fast run or when the head shakes violently.

time in a heavy sea on nylon line, a carp rod and fixed-spool reel, it was well beaten and wallowing a few feet out from the ledge on which Mike stood. A couple of paces seaward and the extra depth of water could have been used to slide the fish on to the smooth rock, but Mike decided to stay where he was and bring the fish over the edge on a big wave. To cut a long story short, he mistimed his lift, the wave receded, the bass head-butted the vertical rock face and the line parted. Not surprisingly, the air was blue. To bait-fish on the bottom over the same rugged terrain where the bass was lost it would be necessary to double or treble the line strength to stand a reasonable chance of landing exactly the same fish.

So, given plenty of open water in which to play a fish, is there any rule that could relate line strength to fish size? A fish with a body mass of 2 lb would have to accelerate at about 30 ft/s (a good clip) to break a 2 lb BS line. Most fish probably accelerate (or decelerate) much more slowly than this, except:

- When they shoot away from a standing start;
- When you try to stop them dead on a fast run; or
- When the head shakes violently.

These are the danger periods for the angler.

Similarly, at the other end of the line, a yank of the rod during a sharp strike can break a line if the rod is too stiff; if the clutch has been incorrectly set and if the fish is too big or presents enough water resistance to prevent it being moved (like hitting the proverbial brick wall).

So just how fast do fish swim? Surprisingly (to us) there has been very little scientific work on this subject and most of the existing information concerns large, high-speed merchants such as tuna, marlin, bonefish or salmon.

In 1941 scientists timed a 60 lb tuna by means of a bicycle speedometer attached to a reel. Just over twenty years later, a similar experiment involved a magnetic tape-recording device and an oscilloscope for analysing results. More recently, the Japanese have used ultrasonic pulsed sonar, again to measure the swimming speeds of various types of tuna. Video films have also been taken of fish swimming in large tanks. Despite all these gadgets, devices and improved technology, we still know very little about how fast fish swim.

Tuna, probably among the speediest of fish species, seem to range from a lazy cruising speed of about 3 ft/s (about 2 mph or a slow walk) to 75 ft/s (well over 50 mph) in hunting mode or when they are about to hit your lure (imagine this!).

This fine yellowfin tuna, quite a speedster, was no match for Steve's Stella fixed-spool reel.

Big tuna can reach speeds of about 50 mph – most fish are much slower.

Pelagic open-ocean cruisers such as tuna, sailfish and marlin appear to be the ultimate in hydrodynamic perfection, with every body curve and fin angle tuned, by evolution, to a life spent roaming the oceans and catching and eating other fish. From our experiences, other bluewater speedsters such as wahoo, jacks and barracuda are capable of similar brief spurts of these top-end speeds and may even move faster, but they lack the stamina of tuna which can swim almost effortlessly day after day. Recent observations showed that good-sized tuna of about 3 ft in length normally swam at about 9 ft/s and smaller specimens of 18 in swam at only 6 ft/s. These speeds do not differ much from those attained by a briskly walking angler. However, the fish can then accelerate to their attack speed in an instant, easily outpacing the 0–50 mph performance of any super-car.

Humans are also pretty quick off the mark and because it is unlikely that even these fishy speedsters could accelerate much faster than we can and because the body mass of most fish that we catch is considerably less than that of a man, there is no problem when it comes to checking the effectiveness of your tackle or technique in readiness for that fish of a lifetime.

Just get your fishing pal to rush around the garden on the end of your usual gear (preferably minus the hook) while you play him! A sharp jerk of his arm will simulate a fierce headshake. There is nothing like a good dash of simulation to provide a spot of confidence, as any airline pilot will tell you. We often start teaching youngsters to fish by letting them play at being a fish on various sets of gear. They are instructed to try to break the line by running and pulling. None has ever succeeded.

So what is the best monofilament line for sea angling? This deceptively simple question is probably one of the most difficult to answer. Some line manufacturers produce separate lines for coarse fishing, spinning and sea angling and, if you take a look at the saltwater lines, you will generally find them to be coarser, shinier, springier, less supple and usually cheaper than most other monofilaments, although this is now beginning to change.

The implication of all this would seem to be that sea fish are in some way less sophisticated than other fish, that sea angling methods are somehow cruder and that saltwater fishing is likely to result in very heavy losses of line. In fact, the requirements and needs of the sea angler are no different from those of the most demanding coarse angler or the fussiest trout man. The lines with the best attributes of strength, fineness, suppleness and transparency will be best for every form of angling.

Next time you decide to buy a spool of nylon ask yourself whether there is any merit in buying a cheap springy 'sea line'. After all, the object of angling is to catch fish, not to drape the seabed in a web of nylon threads. Instead of automatically regarding your line as a disposable item, think about how you can minimise contacts between tackle and snags by fishing with an alternative approach.

Of course, any line with a tendency to be weak or unreliable when knotted is disastrous. Some of the earlier versions of invisible fluorocarbon lines were notoriously fickle, although modern ones seem better. Glint and flash are never likely to be assets in any line and the only reason for using highly coloured or tinted lines is if there is a need to make them highly visible to you. We could go on at great length about fishing with decent line, but the most convincing argument is the bite you get while the bloke further along the beach curses and swears as he tries to unravel his reel from a bunch of 'Sea Fishing Special'.

In recent years gel-spun and fused polyester lines have become the vogue. These so called 'braids' are much finer than nylon monofil and have virtually no stretch so they offer huge advantages in detecting bites. When you first use them for lure fishing, every tap on a rock or piece of weed on the hooks feels like the pull of a fish.

Braided lines give huge advantages in detecting bites and hooking fish.

All braids are relatively soft, light and flexible. They are very thin relative to their strength, so they increase casting ranges and allow the use of high breaking strains even with light weights and lures. For similar reasons, braided lines diminish water resistance so that boat anglers trying to reach the seabed in strong currents and deep water can greatly reduce the amount of lead needed (and the effort required to reel in).

> Braided lines make it possible to fish in very snaggy situations.

Where is the catch? Braided lines are very soft and, if you have a bird's nest or tangle which pulls tight, they can be impossible to unravel. All braids are more or less opaque (some are whitish or so-called 'crystal') and may be more visible to the fish than nylon. Nevertheless, despite these apparent drawbacks, many experienced anglers, including us, now use braid as mainline for most of their fishing.

Virtually all of our reels are now filled with braid of 10 lb, 20 lb or 30 lb breaking strain. As far as we are concerned, braided lines are a huge step forward for spinning and light beach casting or uptiding and many anglers now use it for wrecking and speed jigging. The braid has never let us down in any way.

Having said that, standard Fireline, for example, starts off as a shiny charcoal grey in colour and quickly acquires a furry white coating, which can be disturbing for new users. This does not appear to weaken the line at all. The only obvious problem is that the furry line tends to stick a bit on the first couple of casts of a trip (other braids are also subject to this so take special care with your first cast or two). Other than that, the line casts superbly, allows you to feel exactly what is going on with the lure and gives an instant, firm contact with taking fish.

We have now switched to super-braids such as Whiplash and Dynon and they have some advantages (they don't go furry for a start) but take a little bit of getting used to – a reel with perfect line-lay is essential. We still have a couple of spools loaded with Maxima Chameleon monofil (8 lb and 18 lb) but use them less and less as the years go by.

Both of us are occasionally asked questions about braided lines so we thought it might be worth setting down our experiences to date. We have been fishing with braid for some years now. We can't say that we have tried every type, but our attitude to line is that it must be reliable, so if we find one that does the job we are not inclined to change.

The first braided line that we tried was Fireline, having been introduced to it by our pal Stuart quite a few years ago. As it comes out of the packet it is charcoal grey with a glossy, stiff, waxy coating on it and does not look too good (there is now a clearer 'crystal' version), but it has three key features that made us instant converts: it is pretty thin, it is very strong and it has almost no stretch.

We spun with our Fireline for a long time before we tried any other braids. We used (and sometimes still do) 6 lb BS for chub, perch and trout. The rivers we fish in all hold pike so, whatever the line, it is essential to have a wire trace. We tend to make up traces of 15 lb wire with a tiny 20 lb breaking strain swivel tied on at one end. Modern multi-strand wires can be knotted rather than crimped and a non-slip loop knot does away with the need for a link to attach the lure or hook. We have landed trout of more than 10 lb and pike up to 17 lb without the 6 lb main-line even looking as though it might break.

Braid is durable and will last for a couple of seasons of hard work (if you keep an eye on the end section for damage). Make sure the knots are sound and, if you feel like it, reverse it on the spool at some point. Braided line consists of many filaments so hook points (and barnacles and rough rocks) can, on occasion, penetrate the braid, causing broken strands which may be tricky to detect. Worst of all, because the lines are so thin and flexible, they are more inclined to knot than nylon (particularly if wind, waves, tide or poor technique cause loops of slack line). Provided you notice at once and don't tighten the line too much, knots pick out fairly easily. However, should the knot pull tight, it is goodbye to a length of expensive braid.

A nylon trace (clear Amnesia or Fluorocarbon if you prefer it) reduces the risk of a lure folding back onto the braid. If you want to use a nylon trace you won't need a swivel – just tie the braid direct to the nylon using an Albright knot. We give ours 16 turns before we tighten it up carefully. This might seem a bit over the top, but it is very safe and secure and we have seen the nylon sheer easily at the knot with less turns. Mike actually ties a 2 in loop in the nylon before knotting on the braid – a little clumsy-looking, but this avoids any risk of slippage at the knot. A good alternative is the J knot which is simpler to tie and seems equally reliable.

As we have mentioned, these days we use Whiplash or a similar braid. This is dull green and soft (like sewing thread), but it has the advantage of being considerably thinner for its strength than the Fireline. We have 20 lb or 30 lb Whiplash on our spools for spinning at the moment. We are casting further and have lost very few lures in snags since we began using it.

Clearly, the big advantage of braid for spinning, apart from longer casts, is the instant contact with anything on the other end of the line. The lack of stretch makes it possible to hook fish easily, even at long range. We have read of the supposed problem of hooks pulling out because of this non-stretch property, but with our gear it does not seem to be a problem at all. Even with such diverse species as chub, perch, bonefish and mullet the braid appears to be fine. Perhaps if you are using very small hooks (e.g. when feeder fishing for mullet) it could be a bit fierce, but for spinning it is magic. For fishing with popping lures, where the lure is often sitting dead still on the water surface as a fish takes, we think the low-stretch property of braid is absolutely essential.

> Braids can be tricky for novices to use, but a few simple procedures soon iron out the problems.

We have certainly changed the way we handle our gear since beginning to use braid. The first thing to say is that, when you load the reel, it always pays to leave a gap of roughly an eighth of an inch between the final turns of braid on the spool and the lip. The other changes in approach have now become so automatic that we never even think about them, but one weekend we were fishing together when we noticed that we had, without realising it, adopted exactly the same techniques. So what are they?

It is essential to avoid loops on the spool when you are casting so:

- First off, after casting, glance at the reel for loose line or loops over the edge of the spool before you engage the bale-arm.

A fixed-spool reel loaded with 30 lb Whiplash braid. Never fill the spool to its brim when using braided line.

Impending disaster! A loop of braid over the edge of the spool will almost invariably cause a tangle on the next cast.

- Secondly, flick the bale-arm over manually rather than by turning the handle of the reel (your hand will then be in the ideal position for the next step).
- Now give the line a tug to tension the line on the spool and remove any overlapping loops before you begin the retrieve.
- Lastly, try to avoid slack line throughout the retrieve.

Despite these changes to the ways in which we fish, we are convinced that the advantages of using braid far outweigh the disadvantages. Any problems can easily be ironed out with a bit of practice and we would now never go back to nylon again for plugging and popping, or for most other forms of fishing come to that.

REELS

Having written something about lines we thought that it might be worth a few words about reels. Essentially we only use two types – a fixed-spool and a fly reel – although we still have multipliers for the odd occasion when we go boat fishing these days. There are two main aspects of interest when it comes to picking yourself a reel (apart from the price).

Firstly, is it suitable for the job you want it to do – will it hold enough line of the right breaking strain and give line to hooked fish without spinning out of control or jamming up solid? Secondly, will it tolerate salt water (this seems to worry a lot of people and the tackle manufacturers make great play of it in their adverts)?

Fly reels

Let's take the fly reel first. Mike (a fly fishing Philistine and devout follower of Scrooge) has only had a few of these in his fishing lifetime. Initially they were cheap, trout-size ones with just a two-way ratchet and no other drag. All of them were used in the harshest possible conditions, often splashed with or dunked in salt water, used to play many fish of 3–6 lb (sometimes even bigger) and given very little attention.

Like all his reels, they were left attached to the rods for most of their lives and propped up in the corner of the room when not in use. Normally the mechanism was stuffed with Vaseline to give it a bit of lubrication and protection, but otherwise nothing else remotely resembling TLC. Rarely did the reels let him down in any way. Over a few years the anodised coating of alloy reels tends to chip and scratch and the metal acquires a white powdery bloom of aluminium salts. This has little effect on the functioning of the reel. So there is probably no need to splash out on expensive fly reels if you just want to try catching a few bass and mullet on the fly, but you might want to adopt a more caring attitude than Mike does and swill your reel off under the tap after fishing.

If you are going to the tropics to fly fish for permit, snook, bonefish, tarpon and the like, it may be worth investing a bit more in the reel. Mike is very satisfied with his Okuma 'plastic' fly reel – a snip at £30 when he bought it. He

Mike's old Okuma fly reel, still up to dealing with a 7 lb bass.

still can't bring himself to spend more than £30 on a fly reel (mean bugger) and he does manage to land fish such as these.

Salt water is very corrosive so a reel made of graphite or hard anodised aircraft grade alloy is pretty much essential for serious saltwater fly fishing and even then they are best looked after or the ravages of the salt water will take their toll. However, we both agree that by far the worst enemy of the reel, wherever you fish, is a spell (even a very short one) spent in a closed bag, box or car boot.

Of course, if you intend to do a lot of fly fishing overseas it is probably a good investment to buy a quality, saltwater-proof product with a silky-smooth adjustable drag. After all, it has been estimated that when a bonefish takes off on its first run, the reel's spool is rotating at something like 4,000 rpm.

Many modern fly reels have a large arbor design, which helps to recover line quickly if a fish runs towards the angler and the larger diameter of the spool drum also minimises fly line 'memory' which causes troublesome coils in the fly line if it is wound onto a small diameter centre spindle.

You may also need a fair amount of backing to give you a chance of landing a bonefish or similar and nowadays gel-spun backing is all the rage. Much like the braid we use for spinning, backing line is incredibly thin and strong and you can load 200 yards on to most fly reels. Our view is that if a fish manages to take a fly line and 200 yards of backing, then we'd be wishing we were using heavier, spinning gear.

Fixed-spool reels

Mike's main fixed-spool reels until a few years back were two Shimano 6010 baitrunners. To be frank, he rarely used the baitrunner facility, even when after carp, and says he would have been just as happy without it. The baitrunners have been replaced with Shimano Stradic 4000s – probably now superseded by the Exage RB or something else (reel manufacturers are always changing models). It has no baitrunner, is smaller, lighter weight and is less subject to corrosion than the originals. These are purpose-designed spinning reels, yet we have also used them when float fishing for wrasse and bait fishing for bass. We use them to catch carp, perch and pike in freshwater too, so they are pretty adaptable pieces of kit and suit most of the fishing that we do, including overseas.

The reels (4000s) are about the right size for our spinning rods (not too heavy or bulky) and the main spools hold far more line than is ever needed in the UK (the spare spool is often lacking in this respect). The clutch or drag appears to be pretty reliable, the roller seems to put up with braided line and the bale-arm return

> Fixed-spool reels are capable of playing very large and powerful fish.

mechanism is effective (we always flick it over by hand after casting anyway – this makes sure that the braid is tidy on the spool before retrieving). Before the Shimanos we both used to employ ABU Cardinal 77s or Mitchell 300s for most of our sea fishing from the shore and they were also pretty reliable (probably because they were so basic). By having two identical reels, if one packs in, it

Fly reel – quality comes at a price. This is Steve's Abel, although Mike, being mean, sticks to his old Okuma.

Steve is into a giant trevally. The gear matches the fish, but it is still hard work.

can be used as spares for its mate, which could be especially handy if you are fishing in remote places.

Everyone is entitled to his or her own opinions and when it comes to sea angling there seems to be no lack of viewpoints. Some years ago we read in a beautifully illustrated magazine article dealing with conger fishing from the shore that 'fixed-spool reels are only suitable for dealing with small eels' with the follow-up comment, 'I like to have a reserve of power that only a good multiplier gives'. Now the angler writing this article was very experienced and may well have good cause to use the tackle he described – multiplier reel, 12 ft beach caster and 30 lb line – but to suggest that a fixed-spool reel can't cope with big fish of any species is totally misleading.

The first point to make is that large coarse and game fish are landed every week by anglers using quite small fixed-spool reels and it is certainly not true that conger or any other shore-caught fish have 'more go' than pike, carp or salmon. We have landed all four species on similar tackle – fixed-spool reels loaded with lines of 10–20 lb BS – and although each fish fights in its own characteristic fashion, it is equally possible to play, tire and land them all by proper use of the gear.

Once the hook has found its mark, the object of the exercise should be to keep as much pressure on the fish as the line-strength and hook hold will allow. When the fish runs, the tension is applied by means of a clutch or drag, by applying finger or palm pressure to the spool, or a combination of both. In our opinion, the most important part of any reel is the drag, which must give line smoothly when required. A stiff or ill-set drag can cause the loss of fish, so the drag should be pre-tensioned, according to a number of factors:

- The breaking strain of the line;
- The test curve or, more aptly, the 'stiffness' of the rod;
- The size and strength of the hook(s) you are trying to set.

If the fish threatens to attain the sanctuary of snags or to strip off too much line then, by clamping down on the spool, loss of line can usually be stopped

The Mexican roosterfish is one of many tropical species that will test your drag.

instantly, whatever the nature of the reel. Of course, such tactics are generally a last resort and often end in something giving under the strain.

When the chance arises to recover line this is achieved most efficiently by some form of pumping, i.e. drawing the fish towards the shore or boat by raising the rod, followed by a smooth retrieve of the line as the rod is lowered for the next haul. Again, the nature of the reel is irrelevant.

There have been times though, when one of us has hooked an unstoppable train of a fish and had to watch helplessly as the line disappeared down to the knot on the spool. There is perhaps no worse feeling than losing a 'fish of a lifetime'.

Having suffered this indignity once too often, we have recently both taken to using high-end fixed-spool reels for our holiday fishing trips to tropical climes. The main features of these reels are the quality of the materials used in the construction, which hopefully infers a high degree of reliability and the amount of stopping power or 'drag' that can be applied to subdue big, powerful fish. Such reels have all of the hauling ability of a medium sized multiplier and are capable of taming 100 lb tuna, stubborn giant trevally and huge acrobatic tarpon.

Admittedly, there may be situations such as casting heavy leads to the horizon or winching even heavier leads from the seabed when fixed-spool reels are not ideal or even mechanically strong enough to do the job. However, when it comes to landing that 70 lb conger from the shore, we have no qualms about the capabilities of a fixed-spool reel. If the fish escapes it will almost certainly be our fault!

chapter_**11**

HOOKS AND WEIGHTS
THE VITAL LINKS

FISH HOOKS

Forged, snecked, beaked, plated, circled and chemically sharpened: these are just a few of the adjectives applied to modern hooks. Every serious angler has his own preference, but does it make any difference to the number of fish actually landed? The very fact that there are so many different hook patterns suggests that there is no ideal hook and that, perhaps on most occasions, it does not really matter very much which pattern is on the end of the line. So what are the criteria that should be applied to hook choice?

Firstly, a hook must be small enough to fit within the mouth of the chosen quarry. This may be critical if the fish you have in mind are small in the mouth, either because they are very young, because they are small fish or even because they are large fish that happen to be blessed with tiny mouths.

> There is no ideal hook for all purposes.

Some flatfishes and breams are notable examples. It is amazing how fish with very small mouths can sometimes absorb massive lumps of bait and metal, but, on the whole, it is best to fit the hook size to the fish you are after. Fish such as mullet have quite large mouths, but because of the delicate mouth membranes and the fact that they lack hard bony jaws and teeth, small hooks usually hold much better than large ones in the tough, rubbery lips.

Secondly, the hook must generally be large enough to avoid being masked by the chosen bait. If the bait is bulky the answer may sometimes lie in a well-designed rig rather than an extra-large hook. Pike, carp and salmon anglers seem to catch lots of large fish by using relatively small hooks. The mouths of these species range from enormous and bony to large and rubbery. In these cases it is not unusual for hard-fighting fish of 20 lb or more to be landed on 'freshwater' hooks ranging from sizes 8 to 20. Very few sea anglers (other than specialist mullet fishermen or matchmen) ever use a hook as small as this.

This gulf between freshwater and sea angling is perpetuated by many tackle dealers. The first question asked of many novice anglers when they approach the counter of their local tackle shop is not 'what sort of fish are you after?' but simply 'sea or freshwater?' If the answer is 'sea' nine times in ten, out from behind the counter come the big crude hooks.

Apart from the above considerations, perhaps the most important characteristic of any hook should be that it permits near-perfect bait presentation. Again, we have a lot to learn from coarse anglers. This aspect is particularly important where bait movement is critical or where the weight of the hook is likely to be a significant part of the total bait weight. If you are using smallish livebaits such as shrimps, prawns or sandeels, a little lightweight hook will often improve the effectiveness of your bait presentation. Sea matchmen have certainly twigged that the correct choice of hook can make a big difference to their catches.

> When using smallish livebaits, a lightweight hook will often improve bait presentation.

> With hard-mouthed species springy hooks may 'bounce' fish off.

Then again there is the matter of hook strength. As sea anglers progress to the use of tackle which is lighter and more in keeping with the size and nature of the fish which they catch, it will become apparent that almost any good-quality hook is adequate to land fish much larger than average. Modern size eight or ten carp hooks are plenty strong enough to land the majority of fish you are ever likely to hook around our shores. Our pal Alan comments that for those in search of big fish, springy hooks (like most Aberdeens, which are a favourite with many saltwater match anglers) are useless and a menace since decent fish may 'bounce off'.

Of course, there are other things to consider. You may worry that the gape of the hook will be masked by a large bait and, indeed, this can be a problem. Circle hooks, for example, may not be very good with bulky, clogging baits and hair-rigging them could be an advantage. A Pennell rig, or a couple of small trebles, may sometimes be a better solution (and result in less missed bites) than a single size 8/0 'meat hook'. This is particularly the case over clean, sandy or muddy seabeds where there is no wrack or kelp to clutch at multiple hook points.

We are not suggesting that there is no place for large hooks in sea angling, far from it. However, it is well worth having a rethink about hook sizes. No angler should feel that (good-quality) hooks ranging from size ten (or even smaller) are unsuitable for sea fishing.

One other aspect of the hook problem is rapidly becoming apparent with the current growth in popularity of fly fishing in the sea. There is no point (excuse the pun) buying expensive

> **Saltwater flies should be tied on stainless hooks.**

materials and spending an hour tying subtle imitations of sandeels, sprats or crabs on hooks that will rust away as soon as they come into contact with seawater. This is particularly important with artificial flies because the dressing materials absorb and retain salt water and compound the problem.

One or two patterns of stainless steel hook are available for fly tying, but there can be no doubt that there is a market for more and better ones. Similarly, the trebles on plugs and poppers are often the only bit of the lure subject to rapid deterioration. This is particularly the case where the hook is dressed with a tassel or plume of hair. We notice that one big lure manufacturer is now selling (at a price) packs of spare trebles for their lures. Surely it is not beyond the wit of modern science to produce a more or less rustless treble hook, rather than a rustless coating that is removed the first time a hook is sharpened. Until then we will continue to carry a little box of replacement trebles (of our choice) for our lures.

Mike is not a great fusspot when it comes to tackle. In fact any of his friends would tell you that he is a bit of a fishing tackle miser, but he considers cheap hooks to be false economy. He takes up the story of hooks for sea fish to consider another aspect:

If I need some kit I tend to pop into the small local tackle shop and buy what they have on the shelf. Of course, I would not buy anything which I thought was unreliable, so even if it costs a bit extra I tend to go for well-known brands. When it comes to hooks Mustad, Drennan and Kamasan are all stocked locally so they are usually the ones in my bag. If I am after small hooks for float or fly fishing for mullet I tend to go for those patterns designed for carp or 'specimen' freshwater fish. These days I also use Owner and VMC trebles and Varivas or Owner circle hooks for bait fishing.

Anyway, to come to the point. Some time ago I looked in my 'dry mullet fly' box (an old film cassette container) to find that I was right out of poly flies ('Ladle's Fancies' as one of my mates mockingly called them) for thick-lips. It was a big spring tide that evening and I was raring to go, so I nipped down to the shop, just before it closed, to buy a few size 10s and 12s. I peered along the rows of hook packets to see what was available and soon found just what I wanted. It was only when I got home and began to whip the first bit of foam onto a hook that I realised that my eyesight had let me down. The hooks were barbless!

Now my logic has always been that barbless hooks were all right for 'poncey' freshwater species such as dace or roach (I like them really), but if I was going to hook a decent bass or mullet I wanted the reassurance of a barb. Anyway, it was too late to get any more hooks so I decided to make the best of it and tied my flies on the barbless size 12s.

The fly rod was set up as usual with a floating 6 weight line and 2 yards of 5 lb nylon and it was with some doubts in my mind that I tied on a barbless maggot fly. The first thing that I noticed as I baited up was that the maggots slid on a bit easier than usual, only a small detail, but first points to the barbless (having said that, they also slide off more easily – not such a good thing). I turned to the sea and, although the tide still had an hour to come, there were fish already feeding right at the water's edge.

I knelt down on the pile of rotting wrack and flicked my little fly out into a group of foraging surface feeders. Within seconds I had a take, the line shot forward and my strike connected with a solid resistance. The head shaking and rushing about suggested that this was no mullet and sure enough a couple of minutes later I slid a fat little bass of more than 2 lb ashore. The hook was firmly lodged in the angle of the jaw, but it popped out with no trouble at all and the fish was returned within seconds – I was impressed.

The fly was adorned with a few more maggots (I always keep a handful in the inside pocket of my chest waders so I can bait up without going back to the tackle bag, which may be some distance away) and cast again. A few minutes later and wallop! Another bass took the fly and fought its way gamely to the beach. In all, I landed six bass in the space of about half an hour and, apart from a couple of missed bites, I did not lose any – amazing! None of the fish were monsters and the biggest went about 4 lb, but I think that most dry fly (i.e. trout) anglers would have been well pleased with such a catch.

The best was yet to come. As I was fishing I scanned the water for signs of bigger fish and sure enough, just by a clump of wrack about ten yards from the edge, I saw some big mullet snouts skimming the surface for drifting maggots. To avoid being splashed by the waves breaking in the edge I paddled out into about 18 in of water and cast towards the milling mullet. For once the fly landed spot on and almost before I could raise the rod to straighten the drifting line I had a take. The fish went off like the proverbial train, straight out to sea. It fought with the tenacity that only mullet can muster and it must have been five minutes or more before I landed it. A 5 lb fish – again the barbless hook had done its stuff without any problems.

I returned the mullet and turned back to the sea to find that the fish were still there so I waded out again for another go. My next customer weighed in at over 4 lb and then I had another one of spot-on 3 lb. By the time I released the third mullet the tide had turned and it was getting quite dark so I packed in and began the mile walk back to the car. On the following day I returned to the same spot with three pals. Of course, I was full of stories about the excellent fishing I had enjoyed the night before, but we only managed three tiny bass between us, all on plug baits. My sole contribution to the tally was a firm pull from one bass of about 6 lb which took the fly, rolled to give me a good view and then came off.

To return to the point (or should it be barb?) of my account, the barbless hooks acquitted themselves much better than I could ever have imagined. I have since landed quite a few more bass and mullet on the barbless flies and I shall have no qualms about using them in future. They certainly stick in well

Closer than you think – these mullet, prime targets for fly tackle and small hooks, were only a few feet out from the sea's edge.

A near 6 lb thick-lipped mullet caught by our pal Nigel. Barbless hooks work well on these fish.

and even in the wind and waves I was able to remain in contact with the fish. It only remains to crush (with pliers) the barbs of my 4/0 Vikings and the VMC trebles on my plugs. Crushing barbs with pliers is certainly better than trying to file them down.

Just one last thing: when you pack in don't forget to remove all the maggots from the pocket of your waders. Maggots burrowing into the carpet and/or a car-full of bluebottles are generally frowned on by your better half.

Circle hooks

'Old Ladle's got another bee in his bonnet! This time it's blooming circle hooks.' Just the sort of thing that you might justifiably think when you read some of Mike's tactics or catch fish blog pages. However, Mike's son Richard recently pointed out a scientific study of these hooks and, would you believe it, it looks as if they actually work.

Firstly we should say that there is nothing new fangled about this type of hook. The first reference that we have to their use is from 1897. A good example of the traditional use of circle hooks is to be seen in New Zealand where many of the Maori fish hooks are circles. Clearly, these bone and wooden hooks are not what you'd call 'sharp in the point'. Rather, it is the principle of the design that works and because circle hooks catch in the corner of the mouth and stay there, they have been a success for hundreds, if not thousands of years.

Most fish hooks are J-shaped. When a fish takes the bait you strike sharply to embed the point and barb in the mouth of the fish. The design is clever and very effective and, provided you are after fish to eat and don't mind killing some of your catch, they are an excellent tried-and-tested design.

In recent years, with the massive decline in fish stocks, conservation has become a key factor in fisheries. With angling being a fairly inefficient method of depleting stocks, not much attention has been paid to the matter of fishing mortality caused by 'rod and liners'. One of the key advantages gained by using conventional rod and line methods is that the by-catch is minimal. Whereas trawls, gillnets, traps and long-lines often cause total mortality of the catch which may not only include many undersized fish but also lots of other unwanted species (fish, crabs, whales, dolphins, birds – you name it), we anglers can select what we want and avoid or put back the rest unharmed.

This is all very well, provided the fish we put back survive. If they are handled with reasonable care, most fish we return do recover and thrive, but anything that we can do to improve this survival is another big plus for angling. Canadian researchers Cooke and Suski recently gave an excellent account of scientific study into the benefits of circle hooks. The gist of the results is that:

■ More fish were jaw-hooked when using circle hooks.
■ Mortalities were consistently lower for circle hooks than for J hooks.

There were a very few examples of circle hooks causing more damage than conventional ones (in little bluegill sunfish) and in others (large-mouth bass)

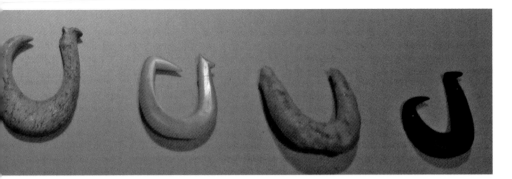

These Maori bone and wooden hooks are not what you'd call 'sharp in the point'. It is the design principle that works: circle hooks catch in the corner of the mouth and stay there.

they reduced capture efficiency and gave no conservation benefit. However, on the whole, they worked extremely well and saved lots of fish, particularly striped bass, tuna, billfish and muskellunge pike.

Circle hooks seem to be most effective when used with live or dead baits. They are probably not particularly good as fly hooks or when attached to artificial lures. However, it seems that in some Pacific Ocean fisheries it is, for purposes of conservation, essential to use barbless circle hooks. Perhaps we should try to be a step ahead and teach ourselves the best techniques for catching fish on these 'new gadgets'.

An email from Chris Teague directed us to another excellent study regarding the effectiveness of circle hooks. An outline of the work is given on a New Zealand kite-fishing website. We will summarise it here and pick out the key

> Circle hooks can be extremely effective, particularly for catch-and-release fishing.

points. We must say that we think anyone who is not using these hooks for bait fishing by now is certainly missing the boat.

The study in this case involved setting long-lines to catch snapper. These are popular sport fish with large, toothy, bony mouths (similar in general form to the mouth of a bass or cod so the results almost certainly apply to fish like these and probably many others). The set lines were fitted with 4/0 or 5/0 hooks and baited with pilchards and the trial involved 60,000 baited hooks in all (you can't say it wasn't a fair test then). On each line the alternate hooks were circles or J hooks (of two types). Of course, there are things to bear in mind about this. Chiefly, that it involves set lines so the fish have to hook themselves. However, since most of the sea angling in this country is still bottom fishing with grip leads, uptiding and/or distance casting of some sort and, because of the nature of these methods, the bait is stationary and the fish effectively have to hook themselves anyway, it must be highly relevant.

To get down to brass tacks: which type of hook was best? Relevant graphs are shown in Chapter 2, but we will quote the detailed results here. In one test the circle hooks caught 507 snapper and the same number of J hooks caught only

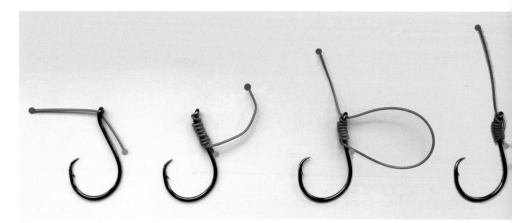

Using the Snell knot renders circle hooks even more effective than usual.

317. This is an increase of almost 60%. Even more significant is the fact that in this test, the circle hooks did not gut-hook any small (12 in) fish, while the J hooks gut-hooked 47 – that's 15%. From the point of view of commercial fisheries the fact that the circle hooks caught small fish (as well as big ones) was a bad thing, but for anglers (particularly match anglers?) this could be a massive bonus.

In addition to the hook comparison, two methods of tying the hook to the trace were compared. Results of this test were even more startling. Circle hooks tied with a Snell knot (see above – we think it's the same as the so-called 'knotless knot') caught 40% more snapper than circles tied with a half blood knot and (wait for it) three times as many fish as J hooks in whatever manner the latter were tied.

As you might expect, when this piece on the circle hook tests in New Zealand was mentioned on Mike's website it stirred up a few doubts in the minds of other anglers. In particular he had a couple of emails questioning whether hooks set on long-lines were a reasonable test for rod and line fishing. We quote Billy Edwards:

Your recent article 'Update on circle hooks' bases its findings on long-line usage in New Zealand. I'm not totally convinced that this is good enough evidence to back up their effectiveness. As I have told you I am from an old Deal fishing family and as a kid used to lay hundreds of yards of long-lines (most of which caught stones of cod and whiting) which used old long shank 4/0 hooks on the end of 3 ft snoods made from that orange hand-line nylon! Therefore I am sceptical regarding this info, because if, as I imagine, there is a plentiful supply of fish most any hook will catch them. We used to catch pin whiting on almost gaff-sized hooks on baits like sprat, whelks and herring (not secured by elasticated nylon either!).

I am very interested in the circle hook theory, as these days any advantage we can get for shore fishing is a well-needed bonus, but will two 3/0 circles provide me with more catching power/options (not too sure these are the correct words!?) if masked with lumps of fresh crab or even three yellow tails?

I have just purchased a few packets and will let you know how they perform when Pennel fishing for cod. I have read all your articles on these hooks and am still not convinced that I am missing the boat.

And Sean O'Sullivan:

You pose the question: am I converted? I'm not sure about that yet. The statistics you post look impressive and firmly in favour of circles over Js but are based on an 'unmanned' fishing style, i.e. rod (or long-line in this case) left unattended for fish to either hook itself or not as the case may be. Circles were the hands down (excuse the pun there!) winner. Do you think similar trials with 'rod in hand' tactics would be as successfully in favour of circles?

We have to say that our own first reaction on reading about the circle hook tests was exactly the same as those of Billy and Sean. Note that although they have doubts they are both still open-minded about giving the hooks a try. Few people can be more sceptical than we are and when a number of people start posing the same question it is always worth another look. At the end of the day, it is only by trying these things that we will get the answers. We were certainly well aware that a hook on a long-line is not the same thing as a hook on a rod and line. As noted above, the fish have to hook themselves and we are sure that Billy is right in suggesting that if there are plenty of hungry fish about you'll catch some of them on any old hook.

However, what we are really talking about is a matter of probabilities. Often one fish caught can make the difference between a blank and a good session. If we can increase the chance of a bite turning into a hooked fish we are all for it. For example, if we use only the sharpest trebles on our plugs and lures, the proportion of missed bites goes down. In the extreme case, surely no one would dispute that you'd be crackers to fish with a lure carrying really blunt hooks.

Secondly, it is certainly possible that if an angler holds the rod, waits for bites and strikes effectively (as we have always tried to do and no doubt Billy and Sean do) then the circle hook may lose its advantage. However, as we said before, many of the modern methods (distance casting, some match fishing, uptiding, etc.) already rely on the fish hooking themselves against the resistance of a grip lead or fixed weight of some sort. This, to our mind, is almost the same as a hook fished on a long-line. So the improved hooking power shown by circle hooks should be a huge advantage for the 'wait-for-a-fish-to-hook-itself' approach.

Finally, whether the hooks are better or not as fish catchers, one thing is certain (and our bass and pike fishing results have already convinced us of this), you will deeply hook a lot less fish by using circle hooks. Anything that saves the lives of fish and helps propagate the 'caring conservation-minded angler' image these days must be worth trying. The sooner we can build up a body of knowledge on the potential of these hooks for angling the better.

Just to emphasise the point, we think circle hooks are a very effective way of protecting and releasing unwanted fish. However, our views have been, justifiably, criticised because most of the experimental evidence has been collected from commercial long-line fishing. More recent scientific work suggests that circle hooks are equally effective when used on rod and line.

This is where the New Zealand study described in chapter 2 comes in. To recap, researchers Butcher, Broadhurst, Reynolds and Cairns carried out an experiment with 75 anglers using a wide range of hook patterns; a second experiment involved fish kept in cages. Overall, about 2,000 bream were landed and released. The result was that over 50% more J hooks were swallowed than circle hooks. Generally the use of bigger hooks also reduced the frequency of gut-hooking. Nearly all the mouth-hooked fish survived. All in all, it seems that a decent-sized circle hook is not only best for hooking the fish that bite but also gives those to be released a much better chance of survival.

For those interested in giving circle hooks a try, Mike has had one or two more emails about their use and the picture is beginning to fill out. Here is the gist of it, edited a bit for clarity. The first one was from Mike's friend Jeff with a question:

I was interested to hear of your experiences using circle hooks for pike and was wondering if you could give me some more details as I'd like to give them a try myself. Unfortunately, livebaiting is banned on the stretches of river that I fish, so I tend to use sardines about 6 in long – a successful bait. Could you advise me on a size/type of circle hook to try, and your preferred method of hooking the bait? I also understand that, with circle hooks, you do not strike but tighten up to the fish. Is this correct?

Mike replied as follows:

You're spot on about the circle hooks. They'd be fine with your sardine baits. I started off with the 4/0s that I used for bass (big squid baits and mackerel livebaits) and they seem fine, but having used size 4s and 6s for perch and caught lots of (lip-hooked) pike on them I'm not sure that the size is too important. You certainly must not strike and I tend to tighten the line as soon as I think the bait is in the fish's mouth (I miss a few small ones). I still occasionally hook a fish in the throat or gill arches, but it is pretty rare. Also, you'll need to get used to rotating the hook more as you remove it – crushed barbs help a lot.

The next email is from our pal John who was already using circles in the sea:

A minor update on the circle hooks situation. As planned, I had a day out yesterday after thornbacks, using one rod set up with Js and one with circles. Interestingly, I caught six fish on each rod, but, alas, results were not as hoped. I had to cut off two circles, as both were too deeply swallowed to retrieve, but only one J. Not a statistically significant test but possibly indicative. The reason I suspect is the manner of skate angling: Angler sees small 'knock' (thornback smothering bait), then nothing (thornback munching bait but static). Angler sees rod tip pulled down (thornback moving off having eaten bait). Angler winds in 'skate' – too late, squid already in thornback's belly! I will try again, but I am not too optimistic.

Lastly, further reinforcement came from Mike's pal Dave:

Today, my son and I had a few hours fishing for spring codling. Using lugworm and size 2/0 circle hooks we did manage to catch a few codling, but also we had eight doggies between us, all hooked cleanly in the lip. Not too bad at all. We also caught a few coalfish – not so good with those: four fish, three deep-hooked. I think bigger hooks may have helped, but they are a very greedy fish. I'm sure we returned more fish than we would have done with J hooks anyway.

So there you are: possibly good for doggies, possibly not so good for rays and coalfish. In the fullness of time we should have some of the answers, but we may never have all the solutions – and that is part of the fun of experimenting with baits and rigs.

WEIGHTS AND MOVEMENT

In relation to circle hooks, we have said a fair bit about static angling methods. The modern grip-lead is now a fact of life in sea angling. Hardly a week passes without an angling writer urging us to 'get a grip'. It may even have reached the stage where some of the more recent recruits to our numbers think that sea angling is not possible without the use of a wired weight.

If you fish the sandy expanses of the East Anglian coast, where strong currents are the order of the day, or if your thing is boat-casting over the sand banks off Essex, then a mini-anchor may be absolutely necessary, but we would like to make a plea for moderation.

What are the disadvantages of a lead armed with wire prongs? Some of them are quite obvious. Any paraphernalia associated with the terminal tackle is likely to result in tangles and wasted time. If the sea is laced with floating weed a weighted grapnel could be the ideal design to rake it up. However, the greatest disadvantage of all, in our opinion, is the one for which these gadgets were intended. They stop the tackle from wandering about on the seabed. One of the most useful tactics in the sea angling repertoire is to keep the bait on the move. By searching the sea bottom with a rolling leger or by slowly retrieving after each cast, it is often possible to bring your tackle to the attention of more fish. It also helps to locate the position of hot spots or 'dustbins' on any stretch of the seabed. Lastly, by imparting movement to the bait you may be able to induce certain species to take. Few brill, turbot, pollack, cod or bass would prefer a dead, motionless bait if presented with the alternative of a lively attractor.

It is possible to obtain different degrees of movement by varying the size and shape of the lead on your tackle. A small lead will be more easily mobile than a large one and a flat-sided pyramid will hold better than a rounded bomb or bullet. So next time you go down to the beach don't automatically reach for your grip lead. Consider whether you would be better to let your bait search the seabed.

On a different tack, at one time the 'lead shot ban' looked like having a nasty spin-off for the sea angler. It seemed that before long it would be impossible for us to get our hands on a sinker that weighed two ounces or less. Indeed, nowadays, small angling weights are all made of various alloys. Our pal Alan is adamant that zinc leads cut the line and says that stones with holes snag less and have some advantages.

We can hear the cry 'so what!' ringing across the water, since many sea anglers rarely use a lead less than two ounces for their normal beach and boat fishing activities. In any case, there are alternatives to small leads, somewhat more expensive than used to be the case, but no doubt most of us get by with scarcely a tremor of the rod tip.

Our own viewpoint is a little more extreme than that of most anglers. If we were told tomorrow that we could never use lead weights again it would scarcely affect our shore fishing (boat fishing might be a bit more problematic). There would, of course, be occasions when we would be frustrated by the need to hold bottom in a strong tide or by the knowledge that the fish were just beyond casting range, but for 90% of the time it would be business as usual.

In no sense are we purists and the last thing we want to do is tell anyone how they ought to fish, but under-weighted tackle is much more versatile. We don't mean simply lobbing a baited hook in to the sea and hoping for the best, although free-lining can be very productive. Ask yourself: how many fishing methods have you personally tried in the sea? As with any form of angling the first thing to consider is what the fish are likely to be feeding on and, consequently, what sort of bait, natural or artificial, is going to be attractive. Having made this decision, how do you get the bait into the feeding area?

> Unweighted tackle allows more bait movement, is less prone to snagging and can often be very efficient, particularly in shallow water.

Surface-feeding fish, for example, may take a buoyant bait delivered on light spinning tackle; casting distance can be increased by using a bubble-float, a self-cocking float or a controller. One of our pals, Bob, created dimpled (like a golf ball), lemon-shaped, wax-filled floats that are amazingly long casting. Kids' bouncy balls also make good floats. Alternatively, denser or bulkier (but still buoyant) lures can be used.

Even the lightest lures (mackerel strip, tiny spoons or plugs) can be fished at or near the surface by using conventional fly tackle. Modern shooting heads or powerful salmon gear will find the fish, even when they are a fair way out and floating lines will keep the tackle on top of the water. In the event of fish feeding deep down sink-tips or even heavy, fast-sinking fly lines may hold some of the answers. If you want to stick to your spinning tackle, again a bubble float or a weighted controller will often get even the flimsiest bait or lure out to the feeding fish.

Mid-water feeders can be tempted from anywhere between the surface and seabed by a number of approaches. These include: suspending a bait under a float; tight-lining to a weight with the hook on a dropper above the bed; using a sinking bait or lure which is then kept up by winding in or lifting with the rod either on spinning or fly tackle; or using a diving vane, either separate from the bait (paravane) or as part of the bait or lure (plug lip).

Generally the thing that limits distance is casting capability, but by skilful use of water currents or wind it is sometimes possible to fish floats, buoyant baits or drift line tackle at surprisingly long range. In parts of the Mediterranean, anglers tether their lines to little rafts with paper sails and drift the baits long distances to find fish. A bit over the top perhaps, but they obviously think that it is worthwhile.

For bottom feeders it is a matter of waiting until the bait settles on the seabed after casting out. The settling process can be speeded up by adding weight, with or without grips. Again, distances are usually limited by casting potential, but in a few situations they can be increased by reducing the amount of weight and drifting the tackle away on tidal currents.

Clearly we have the technology to tempt fish in almost any combination of conditions, wind and weather. Why then do many sea anglers restrict themselves to heavy leger or paternoster tactics? Is it always the best way to ensure a decent catch of fish? Probably not.

Of course, this depends on where and when you fish, but along our part of the south coast anglers have shown conclusively that conventional bottom fishing is often much less productive than methods tailored to catch a particular species.

The question is just how many kinds of sea fish actually pick their food up from the seabed? Probably most species will 'grub about' at times, but a great many of them prefer their menu on the move. Fishing on the drop, sink and draw or just slow retrieve are simply ways of giving the bait life. Often you read about the advantages of fishing a long flowing trace and the movement it allows the bait. Even when the baited hook is hard on the bottom a slow retrieve will attract fish.

We are certain that many readers will now be thinking 'it's all right for them, down in Dorset, where the bass/wrasse/pollack/etc. give themselves up', but, believe me, there are fish keen

> Many fish are attracted to their food by movement.

to take a moving bait on almost every stretch of coast. We have not fished everywhere, but we have had plenty of sport with coalfish and mackerel in the northeast, with pollack and wrasse around the Isle of Man, with garfish, mackerel and scad in Cornwall, with flatties, bass and mullet from Devon, Dorset and Hampshire, with bass, pollack, mackerel and flounder in Ireland, and with jacks, tarpon, barracuda and bonefish in the Caribbean, the Pacific and the Indian Ocean. All of these species and many others, including gurnard, codling, even pouting, whiting and rockling, are live prey addicts and like to take their food 'on the move'.

chapter_**12**

THE BEGINNING
AND THE END
SEA ANGLING THEN
AND NOW

MODERN GEAR

Every year sees a new crop of rods, reels and gadgets in the tackle shops, mail-order catalogues and websites. Things are always changing so we have no intention of trying to tell you which are the best makes or models of rod, reel or, indeed, anything else. Hopefully we can outline the way to choose the most appropriate type of gear to suit the fishing you enjoy. However, when it comes to rods there are so many on the market (and everyone has their own ideas about the ideal rod for a particular purpose) that there is little point in trying to suggest what is best. In general, you will get what you pay for, although, as a rule, it could be foolish to choose a rod without handling it first.

The truth is that we all take our modern fishing tackle for granted. Within minutes of arriving at the beach the very greenest novice can be casting their baited tackle 60 or 70 yards aided by a 10 ft or 12 ft 'spring' of carbon fibre. The reel will be a miracle of modern engineering, releasing a filament of nylon or kevlar from an ultra-light spool, spinning at high speed on almost friction-free bearings or, retrieving via a chain of gears, many times faster than is possible by hand and laying it, perfectly arranged, on the spool. The line, even if it is the cheapest monofilament, will be fine, transparent to the point of invisibility and strong almost beyond belief. Wired grip-leads keep the tackle firmly in place on the seabed. Little coffins of synthetic polymer and cunningly designed clips ensure that the bait remains securely on the hook during the explosive force of the cast. The hooks themselves are barbed and plated alloy, smoothly curved, chemically sharpened to points of molecular fineness and fantastically tough and resilient. The whole set-up, in the right hands, is capable of securing the largest and most powerful fish that swim in our seas.

All in all, we have never had it so good, but hold on a minute. People have enjoyed fishing with lines and hooks for millennia. The fundamental allure and attraction of the sport obviously do not lie in the highly technical developments of recent years. It may be possible to purchase a form of instant success by buying expensive gear, chartering high-powered boats with knowledgeable skippers or by travelling, at enormous expense, to faraway seas. However, the true satisfaction of angling must, at least in part, lie in making a good catch by your own guile and effort. This has been the case for us from those first days when, as kids, we dangled the innards of a limpet into a rock pool to tempt the pop-eyed, aggressive blennies out of miniature caves and crevasses or lowered a decaying mackerel head from the quayside and waited with bated breath for the increased weight and tension on the line which meant it had gained another load of pinching, clawing shore crabs.

All anglers feel the combination of anticipation, skill, luck, suspense and satisfaction, which is at the heart of fishing. Since man first tried to supplement his food supply with creatures from another (watery) world, these feelings have appealed to those of us with the nature to be fishermen or anglers. With all this in mind, we have given some thought to the development of fishing skills. This relates not only to how we begin fishing when we are young but also to how sea fishing was carried out in the years before the development of modern tackle.

IN DAYS OF OLD

No doubt in the distant past, as now, there were some fishers who were more successful than others. However, results must always have depended, perhaps to a much greater extent than in the present day, on the abilities of fishermen to understand the vagaries of season, tide, wind and weather and assess the effects of these factors on the presence and hunger of sea fish if they were to trap, snare, spear or hook them with any degree of regularity.

Just what sort of fish did people catch before rod and reel and how can we find out? About 7,000 years ago Stone Age communities on the west coast of Scotland depended almost entirely on the sea for their living. Widespread evidence of their way of life is to be found on some Scottish islands such as Oronsay. Fortunately, the waste disposal service in those days was not super-efficient and consisted of what we might now call a rubbish tip or midden, handily placed, to receive the waste matter from the homes and villages of these isolated communities. The main items remaining in these middens today are the shells of molluscs, particularly those of countless limpets, which the Mesolithic (middle Stone Age) people are reputed to have eaten.

Broken tools and other rubbish also found their way on to these Stone Age rubbish heaps. A common implement is referred to by archaeologists as a 'limpet scope'. The scope is said to have been used for scraping limpets off rocks, but it seems more likely, to us, that it was for removing the contents from the shells without too much wear and tear on the thumbnail (as all youngsters know, a smart, sideways blow with a handy rock is the best way to dislodge a limpet).

A little more recently (only 5,000–6,000 years ago) clay and stone boxes set into the floors of houses are believed to have been used to keep bait alive. (Tell that to the spouse the next time there are complaints about the dead ragworm in the salad drawer of the fridge.) In these northern waters the villagers used to fish for cod and coalfish, supposedly using limpets for bait. Apparently the Neolithic people were not as stupid as their predecessors and ate the limpets only in times of severe deprivation.

Although the prehistoric fishing lines have not been preserved, they were presumably hand-lines of spun flax (which they used to grow) or the hair of animals. The hooks or gorge-pins, for snagging the mouths or guts of the fish, were made from wood, bone or horn. It is impossible to know whether traps, nets, spears or lines were used to capture any particular species of fish and we can only speculate on the basis of what we know today.

From the town of Hamwic (now Southampton) at the mouth of the River Itchen, there are detailed records of fish remains from about 1,100 years ago. Not surprisingly, the most abundant fish bones were those of species present in the shallow waters of the estuary itself. Flounder, eel, mullet, bass, salmon and even stingray are reported and would have been easily trapped, netted or speared. The use of set lines or hand-lines, involving coarse twine and crude hooks, was probably restricted to the capture of eels, flounders and bass. Gilthead sea bream, quite rare catches even today, were also represented in the rubbish heaps.

It is more difficult to imagine how the Saxon fishermen caught the cod, thornback, whiting, mackerel, pollack and scad that were also found in Hamwic. Equally it is curious, if conventional hook and line methods were in widespread use, that there is no mention of conger, wrasse or other abundant and easily lured fish. The absence of the remains of boneless species such as smoothhound and dogfish could simply be due to poor preservation rather than failure to capture them.

In medieval times, towns in the southeast of England appear to have been dependant on cod, mackerel, whiting and herrings to a large extent. Some change in technology about 1,000 years ago, possibly the introduction of the drift net, resulted in a hundred-fold increase in the amount of herring remains in some excavations. A complete list of species dug up from a site in Great Yarmouth by archaeologists Wheeler and Jones included spurdog, thornback, eel, conger, garfish, herring, whiting, gurnard, turbot, flounder, plaice, halibut and sole – quite a decent range even by today's standards.

The fish hooks from the same excavations were all relatively big and crude and this is hardly surprising in view of the thick lines that must have been in use. Presumably only the larger and bolder biting species such as conger, spurdog, ling, cod, turbot and halibut were caught on hook and line. It is also recorded that eels and flounders were caught on hooks but, as mentioned already, neither are particularly fussy feeders. It is suspected, from the remains, that haddock and large cod may have been much more common in the southern North Sea than they are at the present day (no surprise there then).

All told, our ancestors managed to catch a great variety of sea fish, many of which would be desirable catches to modern anglers. Since their tackle was what we would describe as basic and their very survival depended on what they were able to catch, it is likely that inshore fish were more abundant than they are now and knowledge of baits, times and places to fish must have been detailed and extensive.

Over time, this need to acquire food from the sea in order to survive developed into fishing for pleasure, rather than as a necessity – the sport of sea angling as we now know it – but man's hunter-gatherer instincts are still deep-rooted. We (those of us reading this book at least) have not yet lost our ancestral 'need' to fish in order to provide food for ourselves and our families.

Even many of us who fish mainly for enjoyment and who practise catch-and-release fishing still have that in-built urge to capture fish using the skills and knowledge that we acquire through experience and we all get a rush from being successful. Whether we bring home a meal for our families or a photo of the fish we caught and let go, we all feel the same strong sense of satisfaction that countless generations of fishers have felt for thousands of years before us. Long may it continue to be so.

THE FUTURE: POLLUTION, OVER-FISHING AND DISEASE?

Rubber-booted feet splashed along the rock ledges following the fast receding tide. At the seaward end of the ledge a massive concrete pipe extended into the grey water. On reaching the pipe the anglers set up their tackle and having baited their hooks they lobbed their offerings into the kelpy gully ten yards from where they stood.

It was not many minutes before the rod tip of the most shoreward angler twice jerked sharply. He picked up the rod and, when the nylon twitched and straightened, he struck hard. The fish on the end of the line seemed to have no heart for a battle and within seconds it was flapping weakly on the wet rocks. Its captor viewed his emaciated catch with obvious dismay: a codling of that size should have been at least 5 lb, but this one was barely half that weight.

The pathetic fish was unhooked and returned to the water where it sank slowly from view. Before the sun rose the three anglers had landed ten codling, but only one was a 'keeper'. Five were literally skin and bone, three were covered in cruel ulcers and the ninth, although it looked well, had made their little battery-powered Geiger counter buzz like a demented grasshopper.

For us at least, the above is a vision of hell. Since we were lads, one of our greatest pleasures in angling has been to catch a fish, any fish, which was sleek, healthy and in prime condition. Perhaps it seems far-fetched to suggest a situation where most fish caught were sick or contaminated, but quite a few of the active environmental groups are now painting just such a picture of the North Sea.

Unquestionably, a great deal of pollution enters the 13,000 cubic miles of salt water off our east coast. Roughly 190 tonnes of cadmium, 66 tonnes of mercury and 3 tonnes of polychlorinated biphenyls (PCBs), all very poisonous even in low concentrations, are dumped in to our rich traditional fishing grounds every year. These are only a few of the substances which we and our European neighbours inflict on the long-suffering fish which have for so long provided us with food and recreation.

Although it may vary with time, there is no question that pollution on the scale mentioned above is taking place. Since we started compiling this book we have seen a hugely damaging oil spill in the Gulf of Mexico and a catastrophic tsunami which triggered a radiation leak into the sea from a nuclear power station on the coast of Japan. However, the North Sea is a big place and, without doubt, it can tolerate a certain amount of contamination, so how do such effluents affect the well-being of our popular fish?

Most poisonous chemicals leave the water and stick to the particles of mud and sand on the seabed. These sediments are the food for a whole host of worms, cockles, shrimps, sea cucumbers, brittle stars and other animals, which are in turn eaten by fish. The fish that do most of their feeding on sandy and muddy seabeds are haddock, whiting, rays and, particularly, flatfish such as plaice, dabs and flounders. Due to the association of flounders and dabs with soft sediment, Dutch scientists have chosen these fish as possible indicators of pollution. They claim to have found unusually high levels of disease and abnormality in fish from contaminated areas.

Problems found included wounds and ulcers on the skin of the fish and growths on the livers. The skin, of course, is the tissue that comes into contact with the polluted sand and the liver is the organ in the body that has the job of dealing with poisonous substances.

Of course fish, like other animals, sometimes suffer from illness and disease. Flatfish are particularly prone to skin problems, so even when the seabed is perfectly clean, some flounders will look the worse for wear. When fish are stressed by overcrowding, over-fishing, lack of food or pollution, they will be more likely to show signs of poor health, so the truth is that it is all a matter of degree.

Environmental scientists claim, for example, that in parts of the North Sea as many as 30–40% of dabs may have liver tumours. The politicians and the polluters counter with the argument that 'our' pollution only affects our own coastal waters and that the evidence is not conclusive. It is much the same story that we were told about the cause and effects of acid rain, and no doubt a close replica of what the Japanese inhabitants of Minimata Bay were told before they were poisoned by mercury-loaded fish.

It would be reassuring to think that it just can't happen here, but how long will it be before we are subjected to statutory limits on the numbers of fish which we can safely eat? Already, anglers fishing inland waters in Canada have just such limits imposed on them.

The truth of the matter is probably somewhere between the extremist views. Scientific evidence suggests that the sea is being polluted and the pollutants must accumulate in sediments, in plants, in worms, snails, shrimps and ultimately in fish. However, biological systems can take a good deal of punishment without breaking down and, provided common sense prevails, it may never be necessary to resort to drastic safety measures.

Unfortunately, governments have a history of hiding behind the fog of scientific uncertainty until disaster forces action. Anglers are probably the only sizeable group of individuals who regularly handle and closely examine live fish of many kinds, so it is up to us to be wary and alert. We must not be afraid to let water authorities such as the Environment Agency and ministries such as DEFRA know if we suspect that something is amiss with our catches. They have the expertise and facilities to detect and confirm pollution problems and when they speak, government departments (sometimes) listen. The battle to protect our sea fisheries is hotting up on all fronts and it would be tragic if we managed to achieve conservation measures such as effective cod quotas (are they possible?) or restrictions on commercial bass fishing (in our lifetimes?), only to find that the remaining fish were not fit to eat or so sick that they were not worth catching.

With any luck, none of us will ever see the day when it is necessary to carry a Geiger counter in the fishing bag or, indeed, when every mouthful of fish has to be counted. Nevertheless we should not be complacent.

Starvation

The seas that wash the shores of the British Isles are – perhaps we should say were – among the richest and most productive in the world. In recent times, however, we have seen the decline of seemingly inexhaustible shoals of herring and mackerel, diseased flatfish have appeared in our estuaries and dog whelks, oysters and fish fry have suffered from the release of poisonous anti-fouling materials. Perhaps the warning signals should have been heeded for we now seem to be on the brink of an ecological disaster.

It seems a pity that it is only when creatures bearing fur or feathers become involved that the media and the great British public turn their attention to the sea. The water, sand and seaweed can be radioactive, the beaches may be littered feet-deep in plastic waste, thousands of tons of poisonous sewage sludge could spread over the seabed, gillnets might besiege every river mouth and sandy cove and barely an eyebrow will be raised. However, show on TV one or two poor, pitiful birds with their feathers caked in oil or a sad-eyed seal wallowing out its final gasp on a muddy shore and all hell is let loose. This concern may already be too late.

The present serious situation is a result of at least four effects: enrichment, over-fishing, pollution and disease. The first, and perhaps the most important, of these influences on our hard-pressed seas is the least obvious one. As in many other parts of the world, the English Channel and North Sea are increasingly subject to blooms of algae. The signs include soupy, dirty water, nasty smells, foam at the edge of the sea and even the death of worms or fish in shallow areas and lagoons.

All this is a result of a changing balance of fertilisers and other chemicals washed in from rivers, streams and sewers. Such enrichment causes tough inedible algae to flourish at the expense of the forms that are the normal basis of the food chain in the sea. Anyone who reads, listens to radio or watches television will have noticed that the bird-watching fraternity is agitated (some may even say they are twitching). In particular, our ornithological counterparts are worried about sea birds. It seems that for some years the puffins, razorbills, guillemots and terns which grace so many of our cliff-bound shorelines have been having a rather thin time of it. In the worst years, even the largest colonies of birds fail to fledge a single chick despite the presence of many thousands of adult birds.

The big question on everyone's lips is why? Just what is the cause of this apparent infertility in our feathered friends? The other question, which was recently put to us by a sea angling acquaintance, is: why should it bother me? As he said, 'The less birds there are to eat the fish – the more fish there will be left for me to catch!' On the face of it, this is a perfectly reasonable comment, but, as always, things are not as simple as they seem.

Sandeels are at the root of the matter. It is said that there are not enough of the little green and silver fish left to feed the hordes of sea birds. The sandeels which inhabit our seas are the staple food of several common sea birds, but why should they be in such short supply? It seems that the declines of herring, mackerel, pilchards and the like, caused by the vagaries of the climate and the impact of over-fishing, have forced commercial fleets to move down the food chain and sweep up vast numbers of sandeels for use as fish meal or even for fuel in power stations.

If the picture that we have painted is even partly correct, the implications are terrifying. Every angler knows that the presence of birds working over the surface of the sea is a prime indicator of good fishing potential. For every sandeel seized by a plunging tern, ten, 100 or even 1,000 will be devoured by submerged predators. If our feathered friends are having a thin time it must be much worse for the shoals of cod, pollack, bass and mackerel down below.

Of course, apart from the birds, there are also a number of mammals that are equally dependent on fish for their living. Some whales are (hopefully) in the process of being brought back from the edge of extinction and dolphins and porpoises feed on the fish that feed on the sandeels. The loss of a key link in their food chains could prove to be the final straw.

Even more critical may be the position of seals. Pollution of the sea by PCBs and other chemicals has, it seems, affected the immune systems of common seals and, possibly, grey seals. This slight loss of natural resistance seems to have been sufficient to make the animals fall ill with a lethal virus disease. Added to these problems, the lack of food resulting from the sandeel scarcity is unlikely to help the survival of our seals.

Although the seal population may be severely reduced by periodic outbreaks of a rampant disease, resembling the distemper so lethal to dogs, we can do little or nothing about it. Even if we had a vaccine (and we have not) it would be impossible to treat the many thousands of seals. Even more worrying is the fact that curing or preventing seal disease seems pointless. We must admit that we are a little baffled by the public relations pictures screened on television showing biologists 'testing the seas' in areas where seal deaths have occurred. They know only too well what is wrong and it is an almost futile exercise anyway because the seal deaths, like the sea bird breeding failure and foul-smelling algae, are just a symptom of other underlying problems.

What we really need is immediate action to clean up the sea and the inflowing rivers which are the source of so much pollution and enrichment. Sadly, it seems certain that the fish which are the basis of our sport and pleasure must suffer in silence for years to come until politicians realise that the food chain does not end with PCB-loaded cod fillets. We can only hope that things have not already passed the point of no return.

Silver linings

All is not doom and gloom. Things, as they say, can only get better. Angling organisations such as the National Mullet Club (www.thenationalmulletclub. org) and the Bass Anglers' Sportfishing Society (ukbass.com) continue to fight tooth and nail for restrictions on commercial exploitation of particular species. Perhaps the most encouraging thing on the horizon is the recently formed Angling Trust (www.anglingtrust.net), which aims, at long last, to unite the millions of sea, game and coarse anglers under one umbrella with a single voice. As Martin Salter, the Trust's National Campaigns Coordinator, says, their job is 'to persuade politicians and others in power to take action to protect and improve our fish stocks and fishing'. We say: 'More power to their elbow!'

INDEX